THE ICON: WINDOW ON THE KINGDOM

The Icon
Window on the Kingdom

by

Michel Quenot

translated by
A Carthusian Monk

ST. VLADIMIR'S SEMINARY PRESS
CRESTWOOD, NY 10707
1991

The publication of this book has been underwritten by a generous contribution by Mrs. Hooda Germack in memory of her beloved husband John.

Library of Congress Cataloging-in-Publication Data

Quenot, Michel, 1941–
  [Icône. English]
  The icon: window on the kingdom / by Michel Quenot.
      p. cm.
  Translation of: L'icône.
  Includes bibliographical references.
  ISBN 0–88141–098–5
  1. Icons—Cult. 2. Orthodox Eastern Church—Doctrines. 3. Orthodox
Eastern Church and art. 4. Icon painting. I. Title.
BX378.5.Q4613 1991   91–21319
246'.53—dc20   CIP

THE ICON: WINDOW ON THE KINGDOM

ENGLISH LANGUAGE TRANSLATION
COPYRIGHT ©1991

by

ST. VLADIMIR'S SEMINARY PRESS

ISBN 0–88141–098–5

Originally published in 1987 by
Editions du Cerf, Paris
as *L'icône*

Table of Contents

Preface

I am invariably overwhelmed whenever beauty is conveyed by words or captured in a work of art. To speak about poetry, you should be a poet; to interpret the mystery of art, you must fathom the depths and mysteries of its expression. As I begin my introduction, I would like to say how happy I am to welcome this essay by Michel Quenot about the icon.

The book's subtitle calls the icon a "window on the Kingdom." I would even qualify the icon as being a portal open to the glory and beauty promised to us, a grandeur and beauty of which we receive a foretaste within the living experience of the Church. So then, it is within the context of ecclesial life that we must situate the icon, as also the testimony of this essay. Icons derive their origin from the Church; anticipated delights of the Kingdom, they permit us to savor both its beauty and its joy. Sooner or later, in one way or another, they bid us to feast more intimately.

Reflecting the beauty of God and His saints, the icon is at the very heart of the spiritual life of Orthodoxy—should I not say, of the entire Church! For this reason I am divided, even torn; divided between a concern to show here the bond of essential unity of the icon, of its veneration, of its theology within the harmonious faith and tradition of the Orthodox Church, and torn by a more personal concern not to attach to the icon too quickly the tag "Ortho-dox." I seek thus to set forth rather the more vital, organic and universal aspect of the icon. Michel Quenot points out very well that the development of iconographic art, both in the West (until the Romanesque period) and in the East, corresponds to a genuine spiritual experience, to an intimate relationship between the Church's spiritual vision and the icon itself. If the icon is seen as not only beautiful, but authentic as well, it is because it pictures for us—through a universal ecclesial tradition—the holy and eternal face of Christ, God and man, dead and risen, as it is engraved upon the most intimate memory of the human heart. With inundating rays of light and grace, the icon little by little frees itself from all that obcures its dazzling beauty. "My little children for whom I suffer the pain of giving birth until Christ is formed in you" (Gal 4:19).

That Truth of Christ, namely His vivifying presence, we all carry within us. According to the charism imparted to each one of us, we are called to cultivate that Truth which reveals itself to us in its Beauty, its Word of Life, consolation, judgment, edification. In this book, it is the Beauty of God we sense beckoning us, introducing us into His presence; as we stand before the icon, the very Beauty of God invites us to contemplate in silence.

Michel Quenot has sketched a brief yet highly descriptive tableau of the icon's history. From the canons and laws governing its structures, he also analyzes several classical icons, and finally, he delineates various elements of the icon's theology. This last chapter is by no means less important than the others. In today's civilization of profit and of leisure, even that which is sacred tends to become materialistic, commercialized, only to find itself reduced to its aesthetic and archeological aspects.

Within the living experience of the Church, the icon is a sacrament of the Divine-Humanity of Christ. Ever since the Divine Word assumed a material, human nature at the Incarnation, ever since His human nature was transfigured by the light of the Resurrection, and His body—composed of matter—was elevated to participate in the Divine Life at the Ascension, henceforth, both human art and language can be baptized and sanctified in the Church. In the fire of the Spirit they become capable of expressing, for our human senses and our intelligence, the presence of the Most Holy Trinity in Itself and in Its saints.

The icon, then, possesses a sacramental quality of different kinds and degrees. First of all, the very creation of an icon, its emergence from the heart of the artist with a pure and authentic beauty, is a mystery, an ever repeated, ever astonishing miracle. So at the end of a painstaking artistic endeavor, iconographers must know both how to humble and to efface themselves before that which—before the One Who-transcends and judges all iconography. Consequently, the icon acquires a sacramental quality that renders it in some sense autonomous. Not only does the icon reflect the glory of the Kingdom of God, it also encompasses vital spiritual energy for centuries to come—indeed, forever.

In the second place, every icon is ontologically "miraculous," charismatic, charged with the vivifying energy of the Spirit; even though in certain icons the presence of God manifests itself more tangibly and the prayer of the Church is focused there more intensely. The grace of God willingly establishes itself and manifests itself in what is at once the most beautiful handiwork of art and of the prayers of the faithful.

A third element of the icon's sacramentality, the very reason for its creation, is its function as a "mediatrix" in our most intimate, personal prayer. Mankind is a sacramental being by nature and needs the instrumentality of both sacraments and symbols to attain communion with the Invisible. Through the intermediary of the icon, a veritable communion is established between the faithful and the mystery portrayed upon it. The Orthodox Church never forgets the functional "diakonia" of the icon: to mediate, to intercede for the Kingdom of the Holy Trinity in this world, through the sanctification of the human heart.

To conclude this preface, let us not hesitate to recall that in the living faith of the Church, the icon is inseparable from the living Word of God, which it portrays in a language of beauty and of light beyond human words. In the final experience of the Kingdom, the human person will become an icon in the fullest sense, transformed from the hidden image into the glorious likeness of the divine Archetype, thereby communing directly, immediately, with the living Word of Christ. From His side, then, there will flow forth inexaustible streams of praise and grace.

Boris Bobrinskoy

1. *The Holy Theodores.* Mistra (1290–1295).
A church of octagonal design.
(Photo: Michel and Lieselotte Quenot)

Introduction

The icon is in vogue today, something not at all surprising in a civilization where imagery reigns supreme. In keen demand within the world of culture, the icon today inspires frequent expositions, and private collections of icons have indeed multiplied over the past few decades. This fancy for the icon often stems from contrary motivations; proof of this is the interest manifested by both the faithful and the faithless. Some among the latter see the icon as a work of art they can appreciate because of its aesthetic value. Others discover in it an exotic appeal, or sense an irresistible attraction whose origin escapes them. As for the faithful, we must certainly mention those whom Orthodoxy fascinates, and who recognize in the icon the unifying element of a spiritual relationship they share with us. But the majority of Western Christians ignore the spiritual wealth of the icon, influenced as they are by an ever renascent form of iconoclasm, or conditioned by some form of pious art that just appears to be sacred art. A fact not to be ignored is that more and more young people want to know the icon better, and it would indeed be naïve to see this as only a passing fad. Would it not rather be a prompting of the heart, the vague perception of an appealing truth? Before being beautiful, the icon must first be truthful, and all the more so because an image appeals to the heart before it strikes the intelligence. Today, when the human countenance is so disfigured, when racial discrimination persists, when so many people suffer from a lack of genuine, sincere communication, faces on the icons radiating a light that comes from beyond fascinate and beckon us to contemplate. Although they speak indeed of God, they also speak about humanity.

The subject of icons, extremely vast both in time and in history, surpasses the framework of such a limited study as this. Our intention here is to offer those interested in the icon, who may not know much about it, some guidelines permitting them to grasp the essentials. Starting

11

with a brief history of Christian iconography, we shall define the religious principles on which the icon is based, before considering its place among the Oriental Churches today. To determine what an icon is requires not only a comparison with Western religious art, but also a detailed analysis of its color schemes, along with the unifying links between the icon's message and its picture. The analysis of a few classical icons ends naturally with an essay on the theology of the sacred image.

The love of beauty—"philokalia" in Greek—enriches us and fills us with joy. Such beauty streams forth from God—who is Beauty Itself—generating the world with divine energies. In Him alone do we discover the beauty of everything. We must plunge into the silence and depths of our own hearts in order to listen to the heartbeat of a world already transfigured.

Dedicated to men and women in quest of this beauty—as all of us are, by our very nature—this little book speaks about an "authentic visualized humanity." For does not every icon speak about God who became man, so that man might be transfigured into the Divine?

❧ ❧ ❧

Restricting the icon to a mere object of art would deprive it of its principal role. "Theology in imagery," the icon expresses through colors what the Gospel proclaims in words. Consequently, the icon is one of the aspects of divine revelation and of our communion with God. The Orthodox faithful assembled in church for a liturgy establish contact with the Heavenly Church by the intermediary of their icons and liturgical prayers.

In his masterly work *The Orthodox Church*, the renowned theologian Sergius Bulgakov emphasizes that

> …each historical branch of world-wide Christianity received a particular gift which characterizes it: Catholicism, that of organization and authority; Protestantism, the moral gift of intellectual honesty and of life; but to the Orthodox, especially those from Byzantium and Russia, it was given to see the beauty of the spiritual world.

The icon then, expresses what Orthodoxy is, and like the Word of God, it transmits the Tradition of the Church. Hence the necessity to define for others what an icon is.

The term "icon" can be misleading: it has often been misused since the 18th century and still is today, even though we are witnessing a "renaissance" full of promise. But the misunderstanding exists, and we must know how to recognize it. Besides, our Western mentality tends constantly to reduce the icon to a religious "holy" picture (in the Roman Catholic sense of the term), which it precisely is not! Such confusion implies a pure and simple denial of its very essence.

The subject is indeed vast. Of Byzantine origin, the icon came into its own in the fifth century; the Byzantine Empire fell in 1453. Considering also the Slavic people, the history of the icon embraces both countries and centuries over vast intervals of time.

Indeed, the icon is closely connected to the evolution of thought patterns throughout the history of Christianity. The art from the catacombs provides numerous examples. Christology (the doctrine about Christ), iconoclasm, pneumatology (the doctrine about the Holy Spirit) can all be found reflected in the icon, which is dependent upon its "canons" (rules), safeguards imposed by the Church to preserve a theology of the icon.

If art imparts to us a conception of the world, it is primarily a language which is expressed visually. To comprehend it demands an understanding of both its vocabulary and its syntax. More than just a work of art, the icon calls for an art form permitting the transition from the visible to the invisible. Its highly refined structures permit just that; to ignore them would be to deprive oneself of the elements essential for reading the image. To fully understand the icon, then, one must necessarily comprehend its organic unity: artistic, spiritual, theological.

Neither purely aesthetic, nor purely spiritual, the beauty of the icon is interior and has its origin in its archetype (model). It goes without saying that its interior beauty will elude the aesthete because the discovery of the very essence of the icon requires an interior light for whoever contemplates it. One must welcome the Light which is God Himself (Jn 1:9; 8:12), so that with purified eyes, one may gaze upon the splendor of Tabor which transfigures the material world.

Let us preface the pages that follow with a prayer recited by iconographers before starting to work:

O Divine Master of all that exists, enlighten and direct the soul, the heart and the mind of your servant; guide my hands so that I might portray worthily and perfectly Your Image, that of Your Holy Mother and of all the Saints, for the glory, the joy, and the beautification of Your Holy Church.

2. *Virgin and Child.* 5th c., Rome, Sta Francesca Romana.
(Photo: André Held)

1

Basics

1. The origin and development of the icon

Preliminaries

To write a historical survey of the icon goes far beyond the brief essay intended in these few pages. Icons were painted and designed for veneration; their painting seems to be quite well established by the first half of the fifth century. An affirmation of this fact is the arrival in Constantinople of a portrait of the Virgin and Child ("Hodigitria") attributed to St Luke. Whether or not he painted one or more pictures of the Virgin Mary, he is nonetheless the only evangelist to give us so many details about her. Considered rightly or wrongly as the first iconographer, he unquestionably wrote the very first "verbal" icon of her, depicting for us a sort of interior portrait.

The art of the icon is imbued with theology. This art grew already richer from the time of the catacombs, over the centuries of the great Councils and the purifying iconoclastic period. In its stride across those centuries, it involved numerous eminent Fathers of the Church, such as St Basil, St John of Damascus, St Theodore the Studite and many others. Emerging from the new culture of Byzantium, which survived for over a millennium (343–1453), the icon is the result of a synthesis of cultures: Greek, Roman and Christian. Roman art itself benefited from Byzantine influence, and although the Slavic nations cannot be included in Byzantium because of their culture, it nevertheless remains true that their art would not have known the same harmonious development without that determining influence. Both the same spirit and the same technique, found far beyond the frontiers of the Empire, permit us to speak of a Byzantine unity, even while recognizing typically national influences.

Before continuing on to the art of the first Christians properly speaking, a quick retrospective in history will permit us a better grasp of its evolution.

Judaism

The rejection by Judaism of any kind of Divine representation is explained by the law given to Moses (Ex 20:4). The representation of the cherubim on the Ark of the Covenant does not constitute a transgression, as they were fashioned according to Divine dictates (Ex 25:15). In spite of the fear of relapsing into idolatry, a broad tolerance existed.

The third-century frescoes decorating the walls of a synagogue in Dura-Europos, a small town on the western bank of the Euphrates River, furnish vital evidence of such toleration. There we can see the most ancient, largest ensemble of extant frescoes ever dedicated to subjects of the Old Testament. Yet not a single pictorial trace of the Divinity can be seen there, unless it is the Hand of God, the Temple or the Ark which convey its presence. Consequently, while it may be justified to establish ties between a synagogue and Christian worship, any similar approach on the iconographical level requires extreme prudence.

The Greeks

For the Greeks, to gaze upon the gods led to both insanity and blindness. The cult of statues of the gods was criticized by their philosophers. In fact, the word *eikon* (picture, image) is etymologically very close to *eidolon* (idol).

The Romans

Although the Greeks venerated portraits of the sovereign, the Romans, who imitated them, developed a tradition interesting for our subject. Spread across the confines of the Empire, the emperor's portrait assumed a judicial importance. The portrait amounted to his very presence. Every act signed before this portrait assumed the same validity as one signed before the emperor in person. Given the context, why should we be astonished that the early Christians exploited such surrounding influence? The difference is to be found precisely in the spirit.

The catacombs and the first Christians

The catacombs indeed mark the beginnings of Christian art. It appeared at the very moment when a certain expressionism replaced an art depicting both form and volume of the human body. The search for new ways

3. *An 'Orant' between two shepherds* (detail). End of the 3rd c.
Catacombs, Major cemetery, Rome.
(Photo: André Held)

to express the impulses of the soul in painting was perfectly appropriate
for the first Christian artists. As for the catacombs, let us not forget that
they were principally subterranean cemeteries where people went to venerate their dead.

A forbidden religion, Christianity thus called for a tremendous dedica-
tion to the faith on the part of its followers. Whence themes of images
recalling the martyrs, and from the Old Testament, the intervention of
God in favor of the Chosen People: Noah, Abraham, Pharaoh of Egypt,
Moses striking his staff on the rock bringing forth water, etc. The Old
Testament scenes of the three young men in the blazing furnace, and of
Daniel acquitting Suzanna accused of fornication by the wicked elders,
are often found. Christian artists also chose abundantly from sources of
pagan imagery of their day. Philosophers enjoyed great esteem; thus
numerous works portray sages seated in a semicircle (a scene encountered
in the icon of Pentecost where the Apostles are thus seated) or a solitary
philosopher teaching others. Christianity very quickly appropriated these
models. Is the Church not the custodian of wisdom, with Christ as its
Master, who at once becomes the Supreme Philosopher? To Wisdom, a
popular subject for the Orient, was dedicated Hagia Sophia (from the
Greek: "Holy Wisdom"), that great church of Constantinople built by the
Emperor Justinian I in 537. This church became the very soul of Orthodox Christianity, until the Turks captured the city in 1453 and turned it
into a mosque.

Pagan symbols revived and transformed by Christians abound: seasons
announce the Resurrection; a ship depicts prosperity and also the
Church; the peacock, the dove, the palm tree, and gardens symbolize
Paradise.

Yet Christians did not just limit themselves to adapting symbols that
already existed; they invented new ones, especially from the second century onward. The adoration of the Wise Men represented the admission
of pagans to the faith; the multiplication of breads the eucharistic banquet; the vine symbolized the mystery of God's grace for the baptized, and
so forth.

Let us not miss the point: this art was meant to be didactic. Retaining
the essential, Christian artists aimed at fostering and sustaining the faith
of the neophytes. A symbolic language permitted them to express what

4. *The Fish and Eucharistic bread.* Early 3rd c.
Crypt of Lucina, Catacombs of St Callistus, Rome.
(Photo: Michel and Lieselotte Quenot)

could not be openly portrayed. Within a pagan and hostile world, such art became a sort of secret code, revealed progressively to the catechumens. In fear of persecutions, or of profanations, Christians of the first three centuries depicted the Cross most often by an anchor, a trident or simply the Greek monogram for Christ (℞). Very widespread in the second century, the fish was used as a "rebus" and represented the most important symbol for them. A sign of fecundity in ancient times, then of eroticism among the Romans, the fish became a condensed form of the "Creed." Composed of five letters, the Greek word "i ch th y s" (fish) formed an acrostic abbreviating the dictum: "Iesous Christos Theou Yios Soter," which translates into: Jesus Christ, Son of God, Savior.

It was not at all surprising, then, to find this symbol everywhere, and this inspired Clement of Alexandria, who died before 215, to write:

> Our seal sought to be emblazoned either with a dove, a fish, a ship in full sail, or with a lyre like Polycarp had, or with an anchor... (*Pedag* III, 59, 2)

The thematic and stylistic unity of Christian symbolism from this era is astonishing. It serves well to emphasize the close relationship that existed between the local churches of Italy, North Africa, Spain, and Asia Minor.

The victory of Christianity

Constantine's victory over Maxentius in 312 was attributed to the God of the Christians. It permitted Christianity, promoted to the rank of state religion already in 313, to advance to the foreground of the world scene. Christian art burst forth from the catacombs and replaced art themes of pagan inspiration. Just imagine the upheaval that took place! Christians recovered what had been confiscated from them. Thereafter, artists were commissioned and worked openly for the new religion. The decorative arts, architecture, but mainly painting, all collaborated both in edifying believers and convincing others. The fact that the emperors themselves joined Christianity led to a mass of new converts. Constantine the Great, imitated by numerous sympathizers, commanded the construction of many beautifully decorated churches. Persons visiting these churches were often able to acquire relics, or objects having been in contact with the bodies of saints, so that when the Church accepted the practice of the making of religious images by the end of the fourth century, it only served

5. *The victory of the Cross and St Appolinarius in prayer.* 6th c.
Mosaic of the apse, church of St Appolinarius-in-Classe, near Ravenna, Italy.
(Photo: Michel and Lieselotte Quenot)

to confirm an already widespread practice. Certainly these images fostered the remembrance of those they represented, in spite of strong opposition from theologian bishops.

Constantinople, the new imperial capital, was inaugurated in 330. In subsequent centuries, it was to become the holy city harmonizing the profane of everyday life with the sacred. To the prestige of the Byzantine-Roman emperor, there corresponded in the fourth century a new representation of Christ, no longer portrayed as a philosopher or doctor, but either as a young beardless hero of graceful beauty or as the Master of the Universe enthroned as "basileus" (emperor). We must recognize that with the proclamation of Christ as sovereign of the Christian world and of the emperor as His representative on earth, a strong bond was established between the Church and the State. It was a bond that had its inconveniences. Thereafter, the emperor with no difficulty whatsoever imposed himself upon his subjects and the neighboring states as absolute master. As for the bishops, they were able to promote representations of Christ which could receive the same cult as the portraits of the "basileus."

Justinian

Byzantium was a strategic crossroad between the East and the West. The creation of its basically Christian art was the result of a vast synthesis, influenced by numerous surrounding cultures. As previously mentioned, the sacred image was already a reality by the first half of the fifth century. It existed as such in the reign of Justinian I (527–565), last of the great Roman emperors. It was during his reign, called "The Golden Age," that the Byzantine world assumed its definitive form, quite distinct from that of the Roman Empire. Justinian's empire included almost the entire Mediterranean basin; his avowed goal was to achieve its political and religious unity. Hagia Sophia as well as other churches in Constantinople, Jerusalem, Ravenna and elsewhere, witness to the genius and intense spirituality of that era. According to Egon Sendler, the sacred image received its harmony, rhythm and grace from Alexandria and other Greek cities. From the Orient, Jerusalem and Antioch, came its frontality and realism, avoiding, however, that rather heavy naturalism associated with their art.

The custom of inscribing on the icon the name of the person portrayed was borrowed by the early Christians from a pagan tradition.

Egypt

From this period, it is interesting for us to compare the third century Egyptian funerary portraits painted in encaustic—a special art technique mixing powdered colors into molten wax—with ancient icons from St Catherine's monastery in the Sinai that were painted using the same technique.

Attached to the head of the mummy, the portrait of the deceased, sometimes complete with inscriptions, served as identification. Proof exists that these portraits, discovered for the most part at Fayyum, were painted while the person was still living and were kept at home as a remembrance. The Christians of Alexandria, who attribute their conversion to the Evangelist St Mark in about 70 AD, quite naturally adopted the local art and custom of placing such encaustic panels in the tombs of their hermits and martyrs. One of the oldest icons, that of Christ protecting Abba Mena, abbot of a monastery, is a magnificent example of these encaustic icons.

The Acheiropoietos Icon

In addition to its Roman and Egyptian heritage, the icon originates from yet another tradition which is of prime importance for its future evolution: the *Acheiropoietos* Icon, the Holy Face "made without human hands." It was sent to King Abgar by Christ Himself. Legend has it that the leprous king wanted both to see and speak with Jesus. King Abgar sent a small delegation from his court. While en route they met Jesus preaching in Palestine. Jesus knew that His Passion was near and so could not fulfill the king's wishes. He then miraculously imprinted His Holy Face in a linen destined for Abgar, creating thus the very first icon, source and basis for all the others. Let us note that a western version of the legend also exists: that of Veronica's veil, onto which Jesus supposedly imprinted His Holy Face. There is here an evident parallelism; does not the name "Veronica" mean, "vera icona": true icon?

Modern methods of investigation have obtained a three-dimensional view of the impression on the famous Holy shroud of Turin, whose total mystery can never be solved simply by the radiocarbon dating recently attempted. Looking at it, you see an undeniably close resemblance with the "Acheiropoietos." A strange yet remarkable coincidence!

7. *Christ protecting Abbot Mena.* 6th c.
From the Bawît Monastery in Middle Egypt. The Louvre, Paris.
(Photo: André Held)

6. *Christ Pantocrator.* 6th c.
Encaustic icon, Monastery of St Catherine, Sinai.
(Photo: André Held)

The Acts of the Quinisext Council, 691–692 (Canon 82, Mansi, CI, col. 960), testify to the first official canon about the icon and its importance at that time. They require that artists no longer represent Christ symbolically by the ancient Lamb, but that they paint His humanity, to manifest the Incarnation through which He redeemed the world.

Use of the word "icon" is perhaps most appropriate from that moment in history where sacred images became an object of veneration for the entire Church. This was already so at the beginning of the eighth century, when fervor sometimes bordered on superstition, to the point that the icon of a deceased saint could become the godparent of a newly baptized person. In Byzantium, certain faithful, before eating the eucharistic bread, went so far as to place it first on an icon! Needless to say, such abusive practices were quickly condemned.

The crisis of Iconoclasm

The opposition to the cult of icons had been sporadic up to the eighth century, although it was aggravated by the iconoclasm among the Jews and many Muslim Arabs from the Eastern provinces. It broke out at this point in history with a huge upheaval provoked by the Isaurian Byzantine Emperor, Leo III. Rejecting any representation of Christ and His saints, he felt that such representations should not be objects of veneration. Today, we are forced to recognize that numerous economic and political reasons exerted their influence behind the scenes on that crisis, whose consequences were incalculable.

The iconoclastic crisis was in full swing around 730. The Council of 754, which convened at Hiereia near Constantinople, agreed to a formal condemnation of the cult. It denied outright that the mystery of Christ included both His divine and human nature, i.e., the hypostatic union. According to the iconoclasts, His divinity absorbed His humanity.

Despite the resistance of the Church, the imperial condemnation of the cult of images resulted in a massive destruction of icons, which were removed from churches and private homes. Uncompromising, courageous iconodules, among whom innumerable monks, were treated as heretics, imprisoned, tortured and even mutilated. Their monasteries were sacked and burned, their lands and possessions confiscated.

One day, a monk from Nicomedia was summoned before the emperor, who said to him contemptuously: "Stupid monk, do you not see that anyone can walk on the image of Jesus Christ without being disrespectful to his person?" Quick to retort, the monk threw a coin stamped with the emperor's portrait onto the palace floor and responded: "In that case, I am permitted to walk on your face without dishonoring you!" The emperor's assistants stopped him in the act, and the monk was put to death for having insulted the emperor's image.

This new heresy, along with the continued indiscriminate harassment directed by the Byzantine authorities against iconophiles living in the Italian provinces, only hastened the decline of the Empire. It also sowed the seeds of their definitive estrangement from Byzantium.

The Second Council of Nicea in 787—the Seventh Ecumenical Council—was decisive. At this council, the iconophiles sustained the persistent vehemence of the iconoclasts. They valiantly defended the cult of icons with every possible theological argument. Their victory prompted a restoration of the cult of icons, which in turn provoked a final surge of violence at the beginning of the ninth century (813–842), notably during the reign of the Armenian Emperor Leo V. But the monastic world resisted, intrepid and undaunted, until the final victory in 843, the triumph of Orthodoxy (True Faith) over all the heresies. The 11th of March was then established as the Feast of Orthodoxy, which is still celebrated today on the first Sunday of Great Lent every year.

Because of the massive destruction of icons, it is not surprising that so few icons from those centuries prior to the iconoclast quarrels remain. The most ancient date from the sixth and seventh centuries and originate from regions quite distant from Constantinople: Greek and Coptic monasteries in Egypt, St Catherine's monastery on Mt Sinai, Rome, and also from fourth-century Christian Georgia.

As we conclude our brief historical survey, is it not interesting to note that the icon was at the very center of the deepest, most soul-stirring crises within the entire Eastern Church? Unfortunately, the Western Church never really grasped the true dimension of that crisis, which contributed to the alienation of the Church of Rome. The schism of 1054 only added the finishing stroke to a painful and deplorable separation. When all has been said and done, the icon was the focal point of that profound theological debate whose central theme was the Incarnation, the cornerstone of all Christianity.

8. *The Holy Face.* 20th c. by Monk Gregory Kroug
Wall painting, Three Saints Church, Paris.
(Photo: Andrew Tregubov)

The history of icons after 843

Cappadocia became an important center of sacred art after 843. The valley of Göreme, developed as a center of monastic life by St Basil in the fourth century, blossomed with hundreds of churches carved into the tufa sandstone of a rocky, lunar landscape. Rediscovered at the beginning of the twentieth century, these churches present a great variety of themes and styles. The majority of the churches date from the eleventh and twelfth centuries. This same period testifies to an intense cultural life in Byzantium that expressed itself in a flourishing of both art and theology. The Crusaders' invasion provoked by the Venetians in 1204, along with the plundering of Constantinople, emptied the Empire of both moral force and material resources. Painters in large numbers fled into exile throughout the East and to the West, and to the Balkans.

In Italy, a progressive change in the use of icons became apparent after 1054, although Byzantine influence remained quite constant until the end of the thirteenth century. The fall of Constantinople in 1453 and the invasion of the Balkans by the Turks who, in their wake, transformed the most beautiful churches into mosques, marked the end of a prestigious epoch in history. This period coincided in Russia with a victory which achieved final liberation from Tartar oppression, source of so much horrible suffering. Converted to Christianity in the tenth century, Kievan Rus' rekindled the flame of the extinct Byzantine Empire. Let us note that Patriarch Photius, an untiring promoter of evangelization among the Slavs, was also a devout iconodule. From his time on, the diffusion of icons was rapid, and we can find Russo-Byzantine workshops already at the end of the tenth century. With the aid of Byzantine artists, among them the celebrated Theophanes the Greek (fourteenth century), Russia very quickly developed its own distinctive schools of iconography. Andrei Rublev (1360/70–1430), canonized by the Russian Orthodox Church in 1988, merits being considered the greatest of Russian artists. It was Rublev who paved the way for an emancipated style of painting in medieval Russia. Influenced artistically by his master Theophanes, who admitted trying to express in his own painting "the spiritual beauty that his spiritual eyes perceived," Rublev likewise became the fervent disciple of the renowned and venerated monk, St Sergius of Radonezh, whose extensive influence in Russia was unequaled.

9a. *The valley of Göreme and its Cappadocian carved rock churches.*
(Photo: Michel and Lieselotte Quenot)

9b. *Nativity of Christ* (detail). 10th c. fresco, Karanlik Kilis, Cappadocia.
(Photo: Michel and Lieselotte Quenot)

The icon of the Holy Trinity seen today in the Tretiakov Gallery in Moscow is attributed to Rublev; it constitutes his masterpiece, an unexcelled jewel of iconography. The grace of its lines and the delicate finesse of its colors not only portray an intense spiritual beauty, but manifest to us that which the most beautiful theological texts could never convey.

Without forgetting to mention some of the great schools of Russian iconography—Pskov, Novgorod, Moscow, Tver, among others—we should note that the painting of Russian icons attained its loftiest expression between the end of the fourteenth century and the middle of the sixteenth

In broad terms, it is possible to say that the seventeenth century saw the beginning of the icon's decadence. This reversal was connected to the progressive abandonment of tradition, resulting from ever increasing Western influence, which caused the levels of both spirituality and theological research to fall.

A study of the evolution in the decoration of churches will certainly help us toward a better understanding of the icon. The similarity between frescoes and large icons, as well as small mosaics, permits us to make comparisons of considerable interest. Three churches quite rich in mosaics are still in existence today in Greece: those of Daphni, Hosios Lukas, and Nea Moni on the island of Chios, to which we can add the following churches of Salonica: the Holy Apostles, St Demetrius, and Hagia Sophia. Because they were less expensive, frescoes were more frequent. We can still find some marvelous examples of frescoes in Greece at Salonica, Mystra, Ioannina, and on Mt. Athos; in Macedonia at Ohrid, Nerezi, Kurbinovo; in Serbia at Studenica, Decani, Sopocani, Gracanica; in Bulgaria at Rila, Ivanovo, Sofia; in Wallachia and especially in Moldavia (Romania); on Cyprus at Asinou, Lagoudera, Kakopetria; in Russia at St Sophia of Kiev, the Cathedral of the Nativity in Suzdal; and also in Soviet Georgia.

With her great wealth, Venice could afford the opulence of massive mosaics, as could Palermo and Cefalu. Those of the Kariye Djami (the Chora monastery) in Constantinople assume today a rather particular meaning given their presence in an Islamic milieu. It would indeed be erroneous to think that a complete halt in the arts occurred during the Turkish occupation of Greece, Serbia and Bulgaria. The loss was evident primarily on the level of quality and originality.

Mount Athos itself would merit a study apart due to the fact that it shelters Greek, Russian, Romanian, Serbian and Bulgarian monasteries. Numerous artistic influences are reflected, even confront each other there, and comprise a veritable melting-pot. Last bastions against which the waves of our modern world break, the Athonite monasteries today are still faithfully living the Byzantine tradition. They permit an observant, sensitive pilgrim to grasp the unequalled richness of the sacred art inspired by Byzantium. Most of all, the supreme harmony of the sacred chanting, the hymnography and the iconography all combine during the long monastic liturgies to lead the pilgrim to the threshold of the Divine.

If Russia contributed greatly to the development of iconography by assuming the succession of Byzantium at the time of its tragic decline—for which Western Christians are in large measure to blame—its own decline on the theological level, mentioned earlier, had disastrous repercussions, even on Mount Athos. Simply compare the masterpieces of such monasteries as the Great Lavra, Vatopedi, Iviron, Chilandari, Dionysiou and Docheiariou, to mention only those, with the later decadent frescoes of Hagios Panteleimon and the Prodromou Skete. There is no need here to be an expert or connoisseur of Byzantine art to recognize the essential dichotomies involved. Upon seeing them, however, you readily appreciate the wisdom of the Orthodox Church, which is not so much concerned with whether the art work is ancient or modern, but rather that it conform to the truth of iconographic tradition.

A brief word about Coptic iconography

Coptic iconography would merit a study of its own beyond these few lines. Its art was inherited from a completely restructured Hellenic-Alexandrian art; its "Golden Age" occurred between the fifth and eighth centuries. Still rather unappreciated in our day, Coptic icons differ essentially from those of Byzantium in possessing characteristics which resemble those of a popular or "folk" art. They are works of simple, ordinary people: monks, local artisans, peasants, painted by them for ordinary people like themselves. Linked by continuity with the art of ancient Egypt, which characteristically showed a winged soul flying above a body of similar form, Coptic iconography does not try to portray a person's body or features, but the soul. What strikes us above all are the exagger-

10. *Christ in majesty* (*The Last Judgment*). ca. 1030.
Fresco of the narthex, Panaghia Chall, Saloniki.
(Photo: André Held)

11. *Transfiguration.* Late 11th c.
Mosaic, Church of Daphni, Greece.
(Photo: Michel and Lieselotte Quenot)

ated heads (the contrary of Byzantine iconography) painted on stocky bodies whose features are reduced to a minimum. Their eyes are always very large, expressing the interior vision; they immediately attract our attention. As for Christ crucified, He is pictured with open eyes as an evident sign of His immortality and mercy for mankind.

Although the term "Copt" is synonymous with Egyptian, we could hardly avoid mentioning the iconography of the Ethiopian Church, which is also pre-Chalcedonian like the Egyptian Coptic Church, from whom it partially derived both doctrine and liturgy. Ethiopian iconography is linked directly to the Christian art of the first centuries, transmitted probably by monasteries located in the Egyptian deserts, in the Sinai and in Mesopotamia. Its apogee occurred in the fifteenth century; it is an art enriched beyond the Byzantine heritage and the Christian art of Nubia, leading us to suspect here and there influences from India or the Far East. The obvious geometrical accents given to forms, people and garments, characterize a variegated iconography which uses large splashes of color in profusion.

Here, as elsewhere, the image relates the faith of the people and helps us to discern alien influences. We are forced to acknowledge that in each case, contact with the West has revealed itself as being both regrettable and futile, even if other internal reasons also played a role in the pronounced iconographic decadence which still prevails today among the Copts of Egypt and their Ethiopian brothers. May they renew their authentic tradition and rediscover their original art forms which emanate from another world marked by the seal of the Spirit.

2. The biblical and the dogmatic foundations

Is Christ truly God and truly man, One in the same Person? The fundamental mystery of our Christian faith is based on an affirmative answer to this question. Likewise the veneration accorded to the icon. If the Incarnation is the basis for the icon, then the icon reciprocally affirms the Incarnation. To deny the one, you must also deny the other. Consequently the icon *par excellence* is the icon of Christ Himself.

The "pro and con" disputes over the icon indubitably revive all previous heresies. Providentially, they also bring forth profound theological clarifications of inestimable value for Christianity, and these justify the

12. *Virgin enthroned with Child.* Below: *The Communion of the Apostles.* 11th c.
St Sophia, Ohrid, Yugoslavia.
(Photo: André Held)

13. *The Wedding Feast of Cana.* 14th c.
Vaulting of the exterior narthex (mosaics), Monastery of Chora,
Kariye Cami, Constantinople (Photo: André Held).

icon. The decisive victory of the Church in 843 after the long, intense iconoclastic struggle is certainly remarkable, and it has since been considered as the "Triumph of Orthodoxy."

We must not overlook the important fact that an increasing menace of Islamic intransigence toward images only fueled the quarrels between iconoclasts and iconophiles; it also compelled the Christians of Byzantium to establish an essentially dogmatic, one might even say a metaphysical, justification of the sacred image.

As we have recently commemorated the twelfth centenary of the Seventh Ecumenical Council of Nicea II: 787–1987, which proclaimed the legitimacy of icons and of their veneration, it only seems appropriate to recall how much the iconoclastic controversies influenced art in all respects.

The iconoclastic arguments

The argumentation is based on scripture texts from both the Old and New Testaments: the proscription of the Old Law in the Book of Exodus (20:4); and from the New Testament, the First Letter of St John: "No man has ever seen God" (4:12). The iconoclasts also quote a parallel verse from his Gospel: "No one has ever seen God," but they pass over in silence the remainder of the same Gospel verse: "the only Son, who is in the bosom of the Father, he has made him known" (John 1: 18).

The iconoclasts also claim:

- To say that the icon of Christ represents His humanity without His Divinity is simply to reaffirm "Nestorianism,"a heresy defended by Nestorius, Bishop of Constantinople (c †451), condemned by the Councils of Ephesus and Chalcedon.

- On the other hand, to say an icon of Christ depicts His Divinity without His humanity is impossible, because God could never be represented. This is the point of view of the Arians, who denied Christ's Divinity. These were the followers of Arius (†326), a priest of Alexandria who was condemned by the First Council of Nicaea.

- Finally, to admit that His humanity is entirely fused with or swallowed up in His Divinity, becoming just one nature, results in "Monophysitism," a heresy championed by Dioscoros, Patriarch of Alexandria (†454), and condemned by the Council of Chalcedon.

If we pursue or maintain the iconoclast viewpoint, the entire question of images contradicts the teaching of the Council of Chalcedon (Fourth Ecumenical Council of 451), which defined that in Christ the two natures, human and divine, are united "without confusion" and "without separation." Consequently, we witness the total rejection of the icon of Christ by the iconoclasts, because for them it is a material image which either confuses or separates the two natures of Christ.

The major theological arguments in defense of images

St John of Damascus (650–730), St Theodore the Studite (759–826) and the Patriarch Nicephorus (*c* 750–828) are the principal defenders. Their argumentations can be summarized as follows:

- By His Incarnation, Christ put an end to the Mosaic law and the proscription of images. The Old Testament gives way to the New Testament, which reveals to us a true knowledge of God and liberates us from our former inevitable idolatry. The simple word of the Old Covenant is succeeded by the reality of the New Covenant: the Incarnation, the vision of divinity and humanity in the Person of Jesus.

  The Son is the image of the Father, just as Jesus Himself tells us: "He who has seen me has seen the Father" (John 14:9). This theme is often developed in the Gospel of St John and resumed by St Paul, who sees in Christ "the image of the Invisible God" (Col 1:15), the source of creation and of its restoration in a new world. Christ is the icon (the image and likeness) of the Invisible Father. He thus participates in His divine nature, exactly as the First Council of Nicaea proclaimed in 325. Yet, it is only the Holy Spirit who enables us to perceive that image of the Invisible God. After all, were not the great majority of Christ's contemporaries blind, incapable of seeing anyone other than the "son of Joseph, the carpenter?" (Mt 13:55).

  Furthermore:

  > from the moment Christ is born of a Mother who can be depicted, He naturally has an image which corresponds to that of His mother. If He could not be represented by art, this would mean that he was not born of a Mother who can be depicted, but was born only of the Father and that He was not Incarnate. But this contradicts the whole divine economy of our salvation. (St Theodore Studite: *Refutation* 3, ch. 2, sec. 3. PG 99, col. 417C)

By His Resurrection, prefigured in His Transfiguration on Mount Tabor, Christ sanctifies and transfigures all matter, which can now serve to represent Him as well as the mysteries of our salvation.

The Incarnation justifies and postulates the icon. It is precisely by means of the Incarnation that God penetrates matter which He regenerates in assuming our flesh, so that we too become theophoric—"temples and bearers of God" (1 Cor 3:17; 15:49 and 2 Cor 6:6).

> I do not adore matter itself [wrote St John of Damascus], I adore the Creator of all matter who became matter for my sake, who deigned to inhabit matter (our flesh) and who through matter accomplished my salvation. (*On the Divine Images*, PG 94, col. 1245 AC)

Let us not forget that man, composed of both body and soul, aspires toward the spiritual by means of the corporeal!

The Council of Chalcedon indeed spoke of two distinct natures in Christ: "true God and true man"; but the iconoclasts ignored and rejected that teaching of Chalcedon. The reality of the "hypostatic union" cannot be ignored; we must recognize and admit the union of the two distinct natures—that of God and of man, in the One Person of Christ. In the icon of Christ, it is neither just His divinity, nor just His humanity which is represented, but His entire, complete Person, uniting both inseparably and without confusion. In other words, the icon shows us *the Person* of the Eternal Word *incarnate*—and not simply His humanity separated from His divinity.

Logically then, as His image, the icon shares in the mystery of both His humanity and His divinity. The image involves and embraces a spiritual presence of *the Being* represented and thus can become the object of veneration on the part of the faithful. It is not at all the visible, material element that is venerated, but rather *the Person* represented, to whom our veneration is given. The bond between the icon and its prototype does not mean that they look exactly alike, or must be identical. It depends quite simply on the representation of the Person, whose name is inscribed on the icon, so that "the honor rendered to the image goes to its prototype" (Nicaea II).

Compared to the icon of the Savior, the Gospel is His "verbal" icon. To the iconoclasts who, in the early centuries of Christianity, saw no justification whatsoever for the icon of Christ, St Theodore the Studite answered:

IC XC
Ο ΩΝ
Ο ΣΩ ΤΗΡ
ΔΕΥΤΕ ΟΙ
ΕΥΛΟΓΗ
ΜΕΝΟΙ Τ
ΠΡΣ ΜΟΥ
ΚΛΗΡΟ
ΝΟΜΗ
ΣΑΤΕ Τ
ΗΤΗΜΑ
ΣΜΕΝΟΙ
ΗΜΙΝ ΒΑ

Nowhere did Christ order that even the briefest word be written about Him. Nonetheless, His image was sketched in writing by the apostles and preserved for us to the present. So, what is represented on the one hand with paper and ink, is likewise represented on the icon with various colors and different materials." (*Refutation* 1, ch. X, PG 99, 340 D)

"It is significant [writes Ouspensky] that the quarrel over images is situated within the history of the Church at the transition between two periods, with each one formulating a different aspect of the dogma of the Incarnation."

During the first, fundamentally Christological, period, which is that of the Ecumenical Councils, we see the icon "witnessing primarily to the reality of the Incarnation." The second period, stretching from about the ninth to the sixteenth centuries, was a pneumatological period, answering a need of capital importance, that of "the Holy Spirit and His action in mankind, which is the purpose of the Incarnation" (*ibid*). The icon thus vividly illustrates the well-known statement of St Irenaeus echoed down the centuries: "God became man so that man might be deified." The image of man transfigured truly proclaims the action of the Holy Spirit.

Let us now leave the last words to St John of Damascus from his *Discourse in Defense of Divine Images.*

> If you have understood that the Incorporeal One became man for you, then it is evident that you can portray His human image. Since the Invisible One became visible by assuming a human body, you can make a picture of Him who was seen.

> Since He who has neither body, nor form, nor quantity nor quality, who transcends all grandeur by the very excellence of His nature, who, being of divine nature, assumed the condition of a slave, "He thus reduced Himself to quantity and quality by clothing Himself with human features; therefore, paint on wood and present Him for contemplation, who desired to become visible." (PG 94, col. 1239)

3. The place of the icon in the Orthodox Church

The icon in our daily life

If, along with C. G. Jung, modern psychology insists upon the profound need for images in a harmonious and fruitful religious life, then religious psychology places the icon among the essential needs of the Orthodox faithful. Already at baptism the newly baptized is often given an icon of the patron saint whose name she or he receives. Then, at marriage, the fathers of the spouses bless them with icons. Finally, it is the baptismal icon and that of the Virgin which are carried in front of the funeral procession at their burial. Wherever atheism has not yet scored a victory, there, entering the home, the icon offers itself to prayer and homage even before the head of the house is greeted. Placed in honor on the wall, it invites us to lift our hearts heavenward. Icons are thus present in some way at every significant moment throughout our lifetime. Even portable icons exist so we can carry them with us on a journey. Whenever we make a visit to church, it is always accompanied by the offering of candles, lighted in honor of Christ and the saints, whose icons are then kissed, just as a member of the family is embraced.

The icon within the life of the Church

Without any doubt, Orthodox faithful are keenly aware of participating in the great family of the saints. If you look at the interior of any Orthodox church covered with frescoes and icons of the saints, you assuredly no longer feel alone. Both the individualism and the self-centeredness so natural to humanity simply have no reason for existing here, since every prayer becomes a communion with the saints, those elect whose silent, steady gaze still speaks to us of the interior life.

An aid for meditation, frescoes and icons dispose us to contemplate the *Invisibilia.* Conversely, what a sensation of both emptiness and coldness for any Orthodox faithful who enters a house of worship that is devoid of sacred images!

We should not forget that the House of God reflects the cosmic order: the ground level represents our world, the earth; the vaulting the celestial world, Heaven; and the sanctuary unites them both: Heaven and earth. Already in the fifth century, Pseudo-Dionysius the Areopagite stated that the church should be considered an image of the heavenly Church. Therefore, everything within it should orient us toward the Celestial Court, even its frescoes should not picture scenes of everyday life, but rather the spiritual world.

From the ninth century onward, official rules prescribe the choice and disposition of the iconography to be painted on the walls and ceilings of

15. *The Mother of God* (*Theotokos Hodigitria*). 20th c. by Monk Gregory Kroug.
Monastery of St John the Baptist, Tolleshunt, England.
(Photo: Andrew Tregubov)

14. *Christ the Savior*. Early 16th c.
Church of Jovan Kaneo in Ohrid. Gallery of Art, Skopje, Yugoslavia.
(Photo: André Held)
See page 41.

16. Church iconostasis at the Saint Sergius Institute of Orthodox Theology, Paris, France.
(Photo: Nicolas Ossorguine)

the churches. Accordingly, the icon of the Christ Pantocrator, Master of the visible and invisible universe, adorns the large cupola of the church. It suggests a window on Heaven and constitutes the summit within the hierarchy of the imagery. On the vaulting of the sanctuary is portrayed the Theotokos: the Mother of God, our "Bridge" between Heaven and earth. Surrounding the altar like a protecting wall, the apse pictures the celestial liturgy of the Angels on the upper section of the wall, and on the lower level the eternal communion of the apostles. Above the church exit you generally see a fresco of the Dormition of the Theotokos or of the Last Judgment—vivid reminders for the faithful as they return home. The iconography of the saints occupies the remainder of ordinary mural space. The iconostasis, which we shall consider more closely further on, plays a double role: on the one hand it separates the faithful from the altar, which is called the "Throne of Christ"; on the other hand, like a bridge, it unites them to the celestial world.

Those icons exposed on the "proskynetaria," or icon stands, are there for the immediate veneration of the faithful, who neither kneel nor genuflect upon entering the church; instead they make the sign of the Cross—up to three times, in honor of the Most Holy Trinity. Standing, they recite a short prayer with head bowed before the icons, which they venerate with a kiss: first, the icon of Christ, next, that of the Theotokos, and then ordinarily the icon of the feast-day or of the liturgical cycle, placed in evidence in the middle of the church.

Assisting at a Byzantine Liturgy just once helps to understand the prominent place of the icon in the liturgy. Not only is the icon frequently incensed, it is at times carried solemnly in procession. How could we omit the story about Vladimir of Kiev sending off his ambassadors to compare different religions for his "choice of faith"? After having assisted at liturgies amid the magnificence of Hagia Sophia in Constantinople, they returned to tell their Prince:

> We knew not whether we were in heaven or on earth, for assuredly on earth such beauty cannot be found anywhere else. So we do not know what we ought to tell you; but one thing we know well: there God dwells among men who celebrate His glory in such a manner that no other religion on this earth could equal. It is impossible for us to forget such splendorous beauty.

Vladimir converted to Christianity with all his tribal subjects of Kievan Rus' in 988.

That "splendorous beauty" of the spiritual world belongs in particular to Orthodoxy, for which the *Word* (the Gospels), the *Liturgy* and the *Icon* are all intimately associated.

Everything that is taught by the Divine Liturgy, the hymns of the Church and the words of the reader, truly find a luminous commentary in the silence of the frescoes and icons.

As for beauty, it reaches its accomplishment in each of the five senses. Our eyes are fascinated and marvel at the beautiful sight of the icons; copious, fragrant incense suggests to our sense of smell the sweet odor of the Kingdom; at communion our taste is satisfied by the Holy Bread and Wine; our sense of touch is gratified as the icons, the Gospel Book and the Cross are venerated and kissed. Finally, our sense of hearing, like our sight, comes into play in a privileged manner during the liturgies.

In passing, let us note that organ music and oil painting, developed at about the same time, offer our senses both colors and sounds that are sensual and carnal, and thus express conceptions of a world that is foreign to the icon!

Whether Byzantine or Slavonic, the strictly *a cappella* choral music opens the ear of the heart to the sounds of a different world. Like the icon, this music aims at a reality beyond anything physical and seeks to engender a much higher level of reflection, sensibility and awareness.

The Iconostasis

The term iconostasis means simply a partition covered with icons. Of rather late origin, it attained its classical form in the fifteenth century. In the churches of early Christianity, the sanctuary was separated from the nave by a low screen, latticed grill, or a low, solid wall. With the increase in the number of icons this slowly changed. The icons were first hung onto the grill in one row, and then on a second. Finally, we find up to five rows or tiers, thus giving the iconostasis the form that we recognize today. Its evolution and development raised it to the vault, both isolating the priest and at the same time blocking the complete view of the frescoes on the sanctuary walls. The solution was to use on the iconostasis itself the same iconographic plan as for the cupola, the sanctuary and the nave.

Often misunderstood today, the iconostasis should be re-evaluated in terms of the theology of the icon. By no means a barrier, the iconostasis is, positively speaking, the maximal expression of all that the icon can reveal to us visually. Behind it there is nothing to be seen. Why? Simply because the wondrous mystery that is celebrated there could never be situated on our human, visual level, so to speak; such a wondrous mystery is perceived not by human eyes, but only by the soul in communion.

The iconostasis is thus not limited to simply recapitulating the entire economy of salvation for our eyes and our senses, though this is already a fact of great importance; it suggests a spiritual passage into another world which remains invisible to our earthly eyes. In other words, it symbolizes that boundary between the sensual world and the spiritual world. Beyond its didactic intent and purpose, the iconostasis invites us to a spiritual communion with the Celestial Church. It serves to emphasize that essential bond between the sacrament of the glorious Body of Christ, the Eucharist—and the icon, representation of His transfigured Body.

17. A classic iconostasis. (Drawing from Tatjana Högy).

1a

1b

2

3

4

↑
Royal door
The Annunciation and the Four Evangelists
This door, called "Royal," symbolizes the entry into the Kingdom of God.
The Annunciation marks the beginning of our salvation.

The Old Testament Church (period under the law):
1a. From Adam to Moses (The Patriarchs);
1b. From Moses to Christ (The Prophets).

The New Testament Church (period of grace):
2. Icons of the 12 Great Feasts
3. Deisis = intercession. Prayer of the Church for the world.

The essential row: it is the accomplishment of the three upper rows.

Other Saints	St Peter	Archangel Gabriel	The Mother of God	Christ	St John the Baptist	Archangel Michael	St Paul	Other Saints

4. Objects of direct personal veneration: kisses, candles, incense.

The Twelve Great Feasts

In the Orthodox Church there are twelve Great Feasts which weave a precious crown of images around the Feasts of Feasts: the Resurrection of Christ. They synthesize the principal elements of our faith for the faithful and can be grouped as follows:

THE RESURRECTION OF CHRIST
or the Descent into Hades

(Four Feasts of the Mother of God)

1. The Nativity of the Virgin Mary
2. The Presentation of Mary in the Temple
3. Annunciation
4. Dormition

(Six Feasts of Christ)

5.   The Nativity of Christ
6.   The Presentation of Jesus in the Temple
7.   The Baptism of Jesus or Theophany
8.   Transfiguration
9.   The Entry into Jerusalem
10. Ascension

11. Pentecost
12. The Exaltation of the Cross

There are also other feasts which have their own proper icons: The Resurrection of Lazarus, the Crucifixion, the Nativity of John the Baptist, Sts. Peter and Paul, the Mystical Supper, etc.

4. A brief commentary on the Festal Icons

The Byzantine liturgical year begins on September 1st, and not on the first Sunday of Advent as in the Roman Church. The festal icon joins the liturgical texts in announcing the mystery, thus creating a liturgical and spiritual unity. One can truly say that they enlighten and complement each other reciprocally. During the vigil office of a feast, the priest places the festal icon on a stand in the middle of the church. The Great Feasts, among which Palm Sunday, Ascension and Pentecost are moveable feasts, revolve around "Pascha," the Resurrection, the " Feast of Feasts."

1. The Nativity of the Blessed Virgin Mary—September 8th

Everything in this icon bathes in an atmosphere of intense joy. A leading iconographer, the monk Gregory Kroug (†1969), who rediscovered the soul and spirit of those master iconographers of the great Tradition, states in his *Notebook of an icon painter*: "The Birth of the Theotokos is the final preparation of humanity to receive the Divinity."

2. The Presentation of Mary in the Temple—November 21st

Mary is the first and only woman to enter into the "Holy of Holies" in the Temple, she who would herself become the temple of Christ. The icon shows for us the Virgin being called to the sanctity of the Divine life as the High Priest Zacharias invites her to ascend the steps to the altar of the Temple.

3. Annunciation—March 25th

It is here that "the mystery which surpasses the limits of human reason is accomplished—the Incarnation of God" (Monk Gregory). Unlike parents who give birth to mortal beings, the Blessed Virgin Mary received within her the very Giver of Life, who breaks the chain of death and who will give life in abundance to those ready to receive Him into their own lives. This feast is celebrated at the vernal equinox, March 21, when having passed over the equator, the sun moves toward the northern hemisphere, which it progressively warms and inundates with its light. Is it not the impending announcement of another great joy, the appearance and birth of the "Other Sun"?

18. *Nativity of the Mother of God.* 16th c.
Moscow-Yaroslav.
(Photo: St Vladimir's Seminary Press S–303)

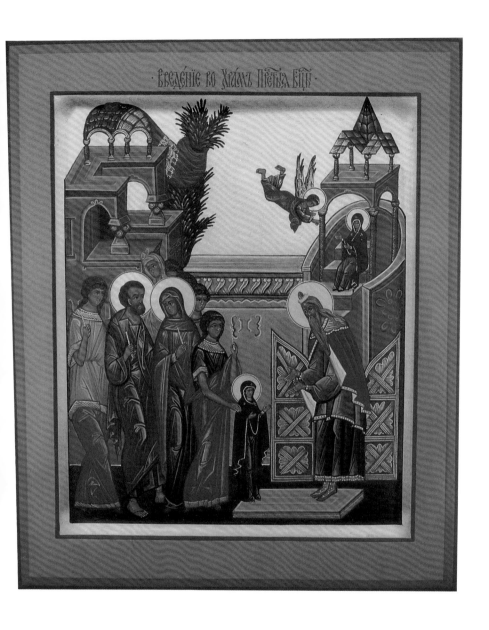

19. *Presentation of Mary in the Temple.* Painted in the 1970's in Russia.
French crypt of the Patriarchal Orthodox Centre, Geneva-Chambésy, Switzerland.
(Photo: Michel and Lieselotte Quenot)

20. *Dormition of the Theotokos.* Russian, 15th c.
(Photo: St Vladimir's Seminary Press S–343)

4. The Dormition of the Mother of God (Assumption in the Western Church)—August 15th

Tradition tells us that all of the apostles gathered together around Mary at the end of her life and that Christ Himself came to take her soul up to heaven. This icon offers a contemplative reading of the liturgy for this feast:

> Neither death nor grave could retain the Mother of God who is always vigilant in her intercession for us, and who is our steadfast hope: Mother of Life, she was transported into eternal life by the Son who was formed in her virginal womb. (Office of the Dormition—from the kontakion of the feast)

The close relationship between the Mother and her Child so apparent in almost every icon of the Theotokos carrying Christ in her arms is, interestingly, reversed in this icon. Her Son, the New Adam, appears in glory surrounded by angels. He holds His Mother in His arms, i.e., her soul which contains her "spiritualized" body. The New Eve whom the Apocalypse describes as "adorned with the sun" (Apoc 12:6) precedes us in her deification, a vivid reminder of those beautiful words of St Athanasius of Alexandria (†373): "God became 'sarcophore'—bearer of our flesh—so that mankind might become 'pneumatophore'—bearer of the Holy Spirit." One might say that the apotheosis of mankind is confirmed here, since both the Resurrection and the Transfiguration, which represent the two theophanic poles of Christianity, find the fullness of their realization in this wondrous mystery: the Dormition of the Mother of God.

5. The Nativity of Christ—December 25th

The black grotto symbolizes total despondency or despair, which is nothing but Hell, the result of man's unfaithfulness. It is there in the midst of mankind's despondency that Christ is born mystically, to liberate Adam and all humanity with him.

Anticipated in the stories of different myths, would not the birth, death and resurrection of Christ be the sign of a nostalgic expectation of the only true Savior? It is nonetheless interesting to recall that Zeus, god of light and the supreme divinity of Greek mythology, was also born in the dark depths of a cave. When you descend into that impressive cavern situated on the plateau of Lasithi, in Crete, you begin to understand the

21. *Presentation of Jesus in the Temple.* Moscow, ca. 1500.
Castle de Wijenburgh, Echteld, Netherlands.
(Photo: St Vladimir's Seminary Press S–315)

22. *Entry into Jerusalem.* 18th c.
Private collection (Photo: Michel and Lieselotte Quenot).

23. *Baptism of Christ.* St Thecla Chapel, 15th c.
Greek Patriarchate, Jerusalem.
(Photo: Greek Orthodox Patriarchate)

phenomenon of how light seems to flash forth out of darkness itself as you look up from such a black abyss at a depth of 70 meters (about 230 feet) toward the daylight of the entrance. Down there, you witness and experience first hand the powerful reality of the icon's inner light and the Light of the Nativity shining in the darkness.

The Byzantine liturgy describes Mary as the Holy Mountain from whom Christ will emerge. Does she not occupy the very center of the icon, lying on a bed of royal purple that emphasizes her dignity as the Mother of God? This event is beyond all understanding and leaves us at first both incredulous and perplexed, like St Joseph in the lower corner of the icon.

For Dostoevsky, "there is only one face in the whole world which is absolutely beautiful: the face of Christ," and "the Incarnation [is] the epiphany of the Beautiful One" (*The Brothers Karamazov*, IV, 1; cf. original text).

This "Winter Pascha" resounds with the presence of Emmanuel, "God with us" (Mt 1:23); and its profound relation to the Resurrection leads us to refer readers to our analysis of the Resurrection icon.

6. The Presentation of Jesus in the Temple or the Meeting of the Old and New Testament—February 2nd

The canopy above the altar table is part of the liturgical furniture suggesting the Temple of Jerusalem, where the Elder Simeon finally met the Messiah. It is Simeon who prophesies the suffering of the Messiah (Lk 2:25–33). The gaze of the Christ-child is concentrated on Simeon, whose whole attitude suggests his welcoming the Messiah.

7. The Theophany (Manifestation of God) or The Baptism of Jesus—January 6th

In this icon, Christ is baptized in the waters of the Jordan. Can we fail to notice here a similarity with the icon of the Nativity? This feast becomes "Theophanic" by the revelation and participation of the three divine Persons of the Most Holy Trinity: it is also the Feast of the Illumination, because the apparition of God is accompanied by a profuse resplendence of the Divine Light.

24. *The Descent of the Holy Spirit.* Novgorod, 16th c.
Castle de Wijenburgh, Echteld, Netherlands.
(Photo: St Vladimir's Seminary Press S–335)

8. Transfiguration—August 6th

The Transfiguration of the Lord on Mount Tabor "is the road to the image, and the summit of the universal Transfiguration" (Monk Gregory), it is not just an isolated miracle. Moreover, we must understand that it is Christ who transfigures Himself for the apostles to see. It is He who reveals His divine glory to the apostles.

9. The Entry into Jerusalem or Palm Sunday (a moveable feast)

The icon is often called a "theology in color." Here is an example from a homily by St Ephipanius of Cyprus:

> Why did Christ, who previously walked everywhere, go up to Jerusalem riding on an animal? To show us that He would be raised up on the cross and glorified on it. What does the town represent? The disposition of the rebellious spirit of mankind evicted from Paradise, to whom Christ sent two disciples, namely, the two Testaments both Old and New. What does the donkey signify? Without doubt, the synagogue that led its life beneath a heavy burden and on the back of whose laws Christ would sit one day in triumph. What does the colt prefigure? The unbridled pagans whom no one could tame: neither the Law, nor fear, nor angel, nor prophet, nor the Scriptures, but only God, the *Word*. (quoted by Monk Gregory)

10. The Ascension (a moveable feast)

The Liturgy of the feast proclaims: "The Lord has ascended…to raise from Adam the fallen image, and to send us the Divine Paraclete to sanctify our souls." A peaceful joy accompanies the promise: "I am with you always even to the end of time" (Mt 28:20). Henceforth reunited to heaven, humanity recognizes Christ as the Head of the Church. In the same way He ascended, He will return again (Acts 1:11) at the end of time. Below Christ, who is pictured in a mandorla of glory, one sees His Mother, and the Apostles who are the pillars of the Church. The whole composition is the image of the Church.

11. Pentecost (a moveable feast)

> When the day of Pentecost had come, they were all together in one place…there appeared to them tongues as of fire, distributed and resting on each of them. (Acts 2:1–3)

The icon shows us the apostles gathered in a semi-circle around the empty throne of Christ, whose divine presence is recalled by the fire and the surrounding light. Below them an elderly king emerges from a black arcade holding a linen on which rest twelve scrolls. He symbolizes the cosmos in a state of captivity and stretches his hands towards the light above, whose source is the salvation announced and preached by the apostles, figured in the twelve scrolls resting on the linen.

12. The Exaltation of the Holy Cross—September 14th

Last of the twelve Great Feast Days, it does not, as some other Marian feasts, derive directly from the Gospels. Its origin is traced back to the discovery of the True Cross in the fourth century, result of the initiative of the Empress Helen, mother of Constantine the Great. The icon depicts for us the Bishop of Jerusalem standing in front of the Church of the Resurrection and presenting the Holy Cross for the veneration of the faithful. The Cross is raised upon "the place of the skull" (Jn 19:17), or Golgotha, in which Tradition sees symbolized the center of the world and the burial place of Adam. The Cross is at once the instrument and the sign through which Christ, the New Adam, frees the cosmos from the darkness of death and grants its transfiguration.

The Descent into Hell or the Resurrection (a moveable feast)

Dynamism and light characterize this icon, which borrows its subject matter from the apocryphal Gospel of Nicodemus. Christ is painted there as the "Living Master of life who holds the keys of death of the the underworld" (Rev 1:18). Having broken and trampled the gates of death, "the Lord extended His hand, made a sign of the Cross over Adam's hand and all the Saints, then taking hold of Adam's hand, arose from Hell: and all the Saints followed Him" (*Nicodemus*: VII, XXIV, 1, 2. Cf. also: 1 Pet 3:19).

"Feast of Feasts," the Resurrection gives meaning to the death of Jesus on the Cross. It explains all that preceded and all that follows. Without the Resurrection, Christian life makes no sense at all. "If Christ has not been raised then our preaching is in vain and your faith is in vain...if for this life only we have hoped in Christ, we are of all men most to be pitied," writes the Apostle Paul (1 Cor 15:14–19).

25. *Exaltation of the Cross.* Russian (Novgorod), late 15th c.
(Photo: Recklinghausen Museum)

26. *The Descent into Hades.* 20th c. by Monk Gregory Kroug.
Wall painting, Mesnil–St–Denis, Paris.
(Photo: Andrew Tregubov)

2

A Study of the Icon Itself

"Beauty will save the world," declares Dostoevsky. To have traveled through Crete and other regions of Greece—that land whose culture has enriched all of us—without mentioning other marvelous places, is enough to understand the impact that beauty has on our senses. This impact finally reaches the depths of our soul which quite naturally turns to God, who is beauty itself, source of all goodness and Giver of life.

Humanity thirsts for beauty! Paul Evdokimov believes that "if mankind aspires to beauty, it is because we are already bathed in its light; it is because mankind by nature thirsts for beauty and yearns to see the Face of God." Without that beauty, our world becomes totally incomprehensible. Therefore, true iconographers have thought only of re-creating that beauty for us. Nevertheless, we must understand this term properly. The beauty of the icon does not come primarily from the finesse of its drawing (the word "iconography" means etymologically: "to write an icon," not "to paint"). Its beauty comes rather from the harmony which emanates from the entire icon, since it portrays the beauty of God and of the Kingdom. It is the result of a long "Tradition" in which meditation and a meticulous elaboration of detail work harmoniously together. The creation of an icon does not spring from a sudden intuition, not from some great emotion, nor from purely abstract ideas, nor from a streak of genius, although the latter is indeed found in many works of great iconographers. In creating an icon, nothing is done at random or by guesswork; all the elements of the process are linked together and form a complete unity. The surfaces of the icon are carefully, even subtly, proportioned for drawing; in fact, geometric lines discovered during restorations of iconographic frescoes leave no doubt as to the minute preliminary elaborations and studies involved.

Interestingly enough, we can note that Plotinus himself, the Neoplatonist philosopher of the third century, spoke about a vision of the world by the inner eyes which would permit us to grasp the profound meaning of things. According to him, the natural reality we experience directly through our senses does not lead us to the heart of things. In agreement with this principle, authentic iconographers do not try to represent external, material reality only, but express as well its spiritual significance. Most naturally then, the result is that the symbolic language of iconography totally escapes the sensual person whose heart is completely oriented to personal comfort and the egotistical satisfaction gained from material things.

Before continuing our study, we must consider the following facts. If we compare the sacred art of the principal world traditions, including Hinduism, Buddhism, Taoism and Islam, we notice that they all have distinct rules concerning their art and its composition.

These formal rules, when added to their founder's personal spiritual vision, help guarantee the safeguard of the tradition's sacred art.

In Islamic art, geometric principles coupled with an ingenious sense of rhythm seek to evoke limitless space—infinity—a symbol of the divine presence. As for the beauty of Islamic calligraphy, which reached its glory in Koranic inscriptions, it proclaims revelation, and is thus analogous with the icon in Christian art.

The same quest for divine beauty also finds expression in the traditional Hindu mandala and in the image of Buddha. In both of these traditions, a canon of proportions is used, from different models transmitted by their ancient masters.

Finally, for Christians, it is the human form of Jesus—the Savior—that is the supreme divine image. Christian art has a mission to help transform both humanity and the world which depends on it. But to do this, our sacred art must conform to Christ and be clothed with His divine humanity.

1. The Canons of iconography: their necessity and purpose

To represent Christ is undeniably an exacting task; but the same must be said about representing mankind, created in the image and likeness of God. We must be careful not to distort the human figure, especially in sacred art, to avoid the risk of becoming caricaturists. To degrade the human face and figure is to insult and to mock God who created them. For these reasons, the Orthodox Church requires that all iconographers conform to an ensemble of Canons, which are at once guides and safeguards intended to guarantee a spiritual continuity and a doctrinal unity that are valid beyond all national boundaries. According to these sacred Canons, the themes of icons are traditional, that is to say, canonically established and defined; they are not simply the result of the artist's personal creativity or imagination. The same must be said for iconographic symbolism. Quite different from profane art, in which symbolism expresses itself by means of allegory, the iconic themes could never be the fruit of intellectual speculation, because the icon directly reveals and reflects the sacredness of the mystery it portrays. Moreover, it "lives" by that reality and can thus be understood only within the spiritual realm, raising a corner of the veil to show us the spiritual reality which remains above and beyond any verbal formula.

The secondary symbolism in the principal details of the icon is easy to understand. This symbolism is varied: from the movement of the hands indicating prayer or supplication, especially in icons of the Deisis, to martyrs holding a cross in their hands, the source of their witness as martyrs.

Clothing styles and their colors are fixed in iconography, as are gestures and numerous other details.

If the seventeenth century in particular offered examples of purely intellectual icons which were strictly symbolic ("the All-seeing Eye," "the Unsleeping Eye"), we must see this as being a departure from Holy Tradition. Both unwarranted and unnecessary, they only validate the basic principles of the true and authentic icon, whose historical course was sealed with the blood of the Church.

In 787, the Seventh Ecumenical Council decreed:

Only the technical aspect of the work depends on the painter; its design, its disposition, its composition depend quite clearly on the Holy Fathers. (Nicea, 6 a, sess. 252 C)

And in 1551, the Muscovite "Council of 100 Chapters" declared:

Archbishops and bishops in all the cities, villages and monasteries of their dioceses will supervise icon painters and personally examine their works.

Thus the first models were established as patterns for future painters of icons, as well as extant works of celebrated iconographers. During this same Council of Moscow, Rublev's Trinity was even proposed as the "perfect example" of iconic art.

Over the centuries, iconographers eventually came to have manuals at their disposal which gave them precise details and instructions about how to paint and reproduce the features of the saints. Without doubt, the most famous manual is that of the Athonite monk, Dionysius of Fourna, which was compiled in the seventeenth century at the request of other monks from the Holy Mountain.

Because the icon provided spiritual orientation for Christian life and prayer, its painting remained a prerogative of monks for a long time. But perhaps nothing was more natural, since a monastery was at once a center and a crucible of the spiritual life; by his vow of obedience, the monk more readily conforms himself to the decreed directives for icon painting. Does he not live amidst the great family of saints, keeping vigils and waxing in holiness, anticipating thus the coming of the Kingdom?

Before drawing the icon on the prepared board, the monk engenders it within his heart in silence, by prayer and asceticism. With purified heart and eyes, he can then draw the image of a transfigured world.

Often the first icon painted by a student iconographer is that of Christ, because this icon in particular affirms the Incarnation. A manuscript from Mount Athos invites the monk-iconographer "to pray with tears so that God may penetrate his soul. Let him present himself to the priest so that he may pray over him and recite the hymn of the Transfiguration." During a period when laymen painted icons and their workshops abounded, the Council of Moscow was very concerned over their moral degradation; it thus promulgated the following decree:

> The painter of icons must be humble, gentle and pious, avoiding immoral conversations and mundane scurrility; he must be neither quarrelsome nor envious of others, neither a drunkard nor a thief; he must practice both spiritual and corporal purity.

When profane influences from the "Renaissance" became too evident, Patriarch Nikon ordered the destruction of decadent icons and threatened with excommunication both those who painted them and those who owned them.

27. *The Holy Trinity* of Andrei Rublev (1411), Monastery of the Trinity-St Sergius.
Tretiakov Gallery, Moscow.
(Photo: St Vladimir's Seminary Press)

If it is true that iconographers should obey and conform to the restraints of iconographic Tradition, which seemingly permit little freedom to their creativity, they should be more than just servile copyists. They must learn to communicate and "translate" their faith, conveying it by their talent. This should be done in the spirit of the traditional Canons, which they must take to heart to enrich and revive. The following words from a contemporary iconographer, Mrs. Fortunato-Theokretov, are of particular interest here and enlighten us about present possibilities in iconography:

> The *raison d'être* of icons is to serve God as well as humanity. The icon is a window through which the People of God, the Church, can contemplate the Kingdom; and for this reason, each line, each color, each feature of the face has a meaning. The iconographic Canon established over the centuries is not a prison depriving the artist of creativity; rather it is a defender and a protection of that authenticity—"orthodoxy"—of what is represented. And that is precisely what iconographic Tradition is all about! When we paint St Peter, St Paul, St John Chrysostom, St Seraphim and all the other Saints, we want to be sure to paint them according to Church Tradition, just as the Church knows and preserves them in Her living memory. On that ground then, there is no reason for us to change the face of a Saint, one of his or her attributes, or clothing or its colors. Nor is there the least reason to change the manner of their representation, just as long as we have not found a better technique to express in painting a body which has become the instrument of the Holy Spirit. Byzantium succeeded in discovering the perfect formula that we still recognize today, and to this very moment every other attempt to express and represent the idea of a transfigured body has failed... As long as the Orthodox liturgy is fundamentally Byzantine, it would be inconceivable that its visual art assume a different manner of expression. (Excerpt from a lecture)

In spite of such fidelity to iconographic Tradition, it is striking to count no less than some forty schools of Russian iconography alone: Novgorod, Moscow, Jaroslav, Tver, Stroganov, etc. And one never encounters two identical icons.

One advantage worth emphasizing is that an icon of any particular Feast Day is immediately recognized by those familiar with iconography.

It is of utmost importance for us to distinguish here between secular art and the sacred, theological art from which the icon originates. This will lead us gradually to single out the criteria of authentic iconography, above all concerning its forms and its content—a necessary step for us, so that we can see the distinction between this art work, which is a transfigurative art, and every other kind of art work, even on a sacred theme, which tries to call itself "an icon."

If Marc Chagall and Paul Klee, to name only a few, have given us a wonderful example of the quest for invisible reality by a very poetic, pictorial language, their art is by no means theological as is that of the icon.

In secular art, the original work and its "worth" reflect the personality of the artist. In a way, it is something like the materialization of his thought and his vision of the world. Public recognition then demands new creations, plus the artist's effort constantly to innovate and surpass himself; furthermore, shrewdly planned exhibitions become a very sly form of publicity. Certainly, these are only a few aspects involved in secular art, but they already permit us to make an initial comparison with the theological art of the icon.

The iconographer nurtures his art both from Tradition and from the teachings of the Church. His personality must efface itself before the personality represented on the icon. The attitude in question is that of the Forerunner, John the Baptist: "He must become greater and I must become lesser" (Jn 3:30), a loving and attentive attitude in the highest sense of the word. As a logical consequence, an iconographer should not sign icons for at least these three reasons. The name is synonymous with the personality, which should discreetly disappear. Secondly, the icon is painted according to a tradition and documents which are not the artist's property. Finally, just to mention the element of "inspiration"—that comes from the Holy Spirit and not from the artist!

If numerous contemporary Greek iconographers give the impression of signing their icons, let us understand that their name is usually preceded by the expression: "By the hand of... ," thus emphasizing the preponderance of their ecclesial ministry, which implies divine intervention.

It is interesting to note that certain secular artists sign their works by pictography, the use of a pictorial aspect within the work permitting their identification. To paint this way in iconography is inadmissible, because those who pray before an icon should not be distracted from their prayer by such personalized artwork. Iconographers must also eliminate their personal sentiments and emotions from the icon, to avoid imposing them on others, thus furnishing an obstacle to prayer. Agreed that authentic, traditional icon painting is implied here—does it not become evident, as one contemporary iconographer has said, that icon painting "is a heroic act and a true apostolate."

2. The comparative evolution of sacred art in the East and in the West

The gradual neglect of the Canons which govern iconography within the Orthodox Church brought about serious consequences. As a result of this neglect, one can notice an ineluctable decline and a slow asphyxia in icon painting. But if we take a preliminary glance at what happened in the West, it will permit us to make quite an interesting comparison.

The sacred art of both East and West expressed the same realities up to the eleventh and twelfth centuries, with an identical impetus that sought to reveal those "things invisible." It was that marvelous period of Romanesque art which unveiled a world beyond the laws of gravity, and even showed us how stone could be spiritualized. Splendid examples of Romanesque are seen at Chartres, Berzé-la-Ville and Saint Savin (France). We must also mention the Irish, Spanish and Italian painting of that era, whose subtle notes were in harmony with the Christian Orient—an Orient whose frontiers, let us not forget, extended well beyond what this term includes today, since at that time it comprised also Ravenna and Sicily. Byzantium was likewise passing through a period of intense life, for we witness a spectacular blossoming of art and of theology, despite the catastrophe of 1204 provoked by the arrival of the Crusaders.

In Italy, however, we see Cimabue, Giotto and Ducio form a vanguard leading to a progressive departure from the art of the Eastern Church and prompting the artistic "divorce" of the Renaissance. Turning their backs on Byzantine tradition, they initiate the "desacralization" of Western sacred art, opening the road towards an uncompromising secularization. The art of the transcendent fades with their introduction of such visuals as three-dimensional perspective, natural light and shadows, the return to a realistic portrayal of people, and use of the emotional—in a word, an art

28. *Christ in majesty.* Fresco painted in 1123.
Church of St Clement, Tahull, Spain.
(Photo: Michel and Lieselotte Quenot)

in total opposition to the hieratic art of iconography. With newfound independence, sacred art ceded to a form of "religious art" void of genuine transcendence. Until then, the icon was oriented toward the faithful, open to them, but it now became a picture living its own life; its scenes took place independently of those who contemplated it. A subjective vision of art, projected by the artist, impaired its integration into the liturgical mystery. Emotions then replaced spiritual communion; and finally, the sacred language of symbols was lost.

We should mention here how fully aware we are that the comparative diagram between "Representations of the Mother of God in Orthodox Tradition and those in the Church of Rome" lacks nuances. Nonetheless, it permits us a much clearer understanding of the important and undeniable evolution within the realm of sacred art.

It is worth pointing out, as does Paul Evdokimov, that the Council of Trent (1545–1563) and the "Council of the Hundred Chapters" of Moscow (1551) were held within the same time span, and yet they came to divergent conclusions concerning the nature of sacred art. While the Eastern Church remained faithful above all to the two-dimensional iconographic surface which is more accessible to mystery, Western Christianity, more liberal, took a different way and opened the door (in view of realism), to three-dimensional sculpture, which is more individualistic and autonomous.

Yet sculptures in relief, though not as frequent as icons, were by no means unimportant in traditionally Orthodox countries. We find numerous high and low relief sculptures of Christ and the saints, particularly in Russia, already in the twelfth century. The Topkapi Museum in Istanbul has a fine collection of such Byzantine liturgical sculptures.

We should ponder the fact that in art the presence or the absence of volume either includes or excludes a solid form or materialization. A choice between the two becomes a determinant factor in iconic art. During about the same time span mentioned above, the Protestant Reformation also opposed Roman Catholic symbolism. As a result, the Protestants covered the frescoes and paintings found in Roman Catholic churches with a generous coat of whitewash. We might as well say that for them the problem of sacred art was simply "conjured away." But we can

REPRESENTATIONS OF THE MOTHER OF GOD IN
ORTHODOX TRADITION AND IN THE CHURCH OF ROME.

11th–12th centuries
ROMANESQUE

13th–15th centuries
GOTHIC

16th century
RENAISSANCE

17th century
BAROQUE

The unity of
Byzantine art.

The variations of
Roman Church art.

29. *Madonna and Child.* ca. 1509.
Lucas Cranach, Thyssen collection, Castagnola, Lugano, Switzerland.
(Photo: Fondation Thyssen-Bornemisza)

find similar reactions already as early as the eleventh century. Let us be satisfied to name only Saint Bernard of Clairvaux, a great figure of Christianity and prompter of the second crusade. Along with the Cluniac reformers, he contested the intrusive art found in monasteries of his day. And what "art" it was! Such pictorial exaggerations seemed to that ascetic monk to be hardly conducive to interior contemplation. This art risked being a mundane distraction for monks, and his reaction to it is still apparent in the austere character of Cistercian spirituality and architecture in subsequent centuries. Whereas renowned Renaissance painters such as Raphael, da Vinci, and others, offer us in their "religious subjects" a beauty that is more physical than spiritual, where anatomical detail, perspective, and colors true to their surroundings are of the greatest importance, an iconographer abandons every superfluous detail, so as to "capture" the realm of the immaterial, the spiritual and the eternal, where both time and space are lost and have no meaning.

We must understand that nothing at all distinguishes the religious art of the Renaissance or the Baroque period from the secular art of the day, except for the "religious" theme. The artistic forms are exactly the same, but the pious sentiments of the artist do not suffice to render it "sacred." An art becomes sacred only when a spiritual outlook or vision becomes manifest in its forms, and when they in turn, convey an authentic reflection of the spiritual world.

If a specific spiritual vision postulates an appropriate visual language or expression, then an art with a sacred theme which reverts to using the classical expression of secular art merits only the name of "religious" art. It cannot be called *sacred* or *theological* art.

It would be at once erroneous and naïve to compare Byzantine iconography with certain schools of contemporary painting such as cubism, expressionism or abstract art, which are characterized by an abandonment of anatomical precision and of that which is natural. It can never be stressed sufficiently: the art of the icon demands a spiritual vision that must be nourished at the very heart of the Church; only then can it become a vision which embodies itself in forms and expressions that will remain faithful to holy, iconic Tradition.

As for examples of contemporary art with crooked heads, crossed-eyes, twisted bodies and bulging bosoms, they express more the "disintegrated"

30. *Virgin of Tenderness.* Russian, late 15th c.
Icon Museum, Recklinghausen, Germany.
(Photo: Recklinghausen Museum)

state of modern man than his thirst for a reality beyond the material world. In such art, where do you find any physical beauty, and—above all—where do you find any spiritual beauty? Is it not rather an art which is a categoric refusal to recognize and consider humanity in the image and likeness of God.

What a contrast between iconography and Western religious art, which remains superficial and is based on living models to represent Christ and His Mother! How many sensually beautiful women, objects of passion for their painters, lent their features to pose for paintings of the Mother of God? Holy texts replete with a spiritual vision describe Her as being the most beautiful, the most pure among all women. She who is so radiant with holiness sees Herself endowed with the natural features of an ordinary woman. What incongruity!

Some well-known examples of this kind of art are found among numerous painters, such as Filippo Lippi, Raphael, Titian and Rubens.

The Sixth Ecumenical Council (680) considers such reproductions as incompatible with the truth of the Faith because of their sensual overtones. To paint Christ as an ordinary man implies the idea of just His human nature, whereas He is both God and man in one and the same Person. The chief task of an iconographer requires the contrary: to emphasize strongly that the fullness of the Divinity dwells in the human body of Christ.

3. A fundamental distinction: the icon, theology of presence

The truth of the matter is this: there exists a profound misunderstanding, or rather, a serious discrepancy between the conception of sacred, theological art in the Eastern Church and the conception of this same art in the Western Church. A visible expression of the invisible, the icon does not exist by itself, since it is a means to lead us to others: to Christ, the Trinity, the Theotokos and the Saints. For the Orthodox, the icon is a true sacramental of a *personal presence,* as the great Council of 869–870 declared: "What the Gospel proclaims to us by words, the icon also proclaims and renders present for us by color."

United for over ten centuries, our sister Churches were progressively to separate and to develop divergent opinions about the essential element of the icon: its *theology of "presence."*

Another important distinction not to be overlooked is the fact that the art of the Eastern Church, imitated by Romanesque art, devoted itself to celebrating the glory of God, the dignity of Christ victorious over suffering and death, while the Western Church remained attached to the foot of the Cross. As an example of this fact, compare a Byzantine Pantocrator or the triumphant Christ of Vezelay, or also of La Charité-sur-Loire, with the Grünewald reredos.

Certainly, we must recognize in that fact a consequence of the impact on the Crusaders of the sight of the Holy Land and the tomb of Christ. The Eastern Christians had always lived in the vicinity of these sites and quickly penetrated the tragic element involved to pass beyond the particular phenomenon. For us, the icon of the crucifixion reflects neither sadness nor abandon, but witnesses above all to a noble presence.

On the contrary, what feeling of emptiness stirs within our hearts when we gaze for a while at the famous Renaissance altarpiece of Grünewald, which expresses so brutally the subjection of Him who assumed our human nature. In the Orthodox crucifixion you can sense the divine presence, while the art of the altarpiece accentuates its absence!

The crucified Jesus of the icon does not have clenched, convulsive hands; one sees a noble majesty and serenity dominating the scene rather than the suffering of martyrdom. "I look at Christ crucified and see the King," exclaimed Saint John Chrysostom. The wide open arms, the head inclined to the side, and the curved body illustrate quite well the consummation of the sacrifice of the Cross declared in His last words: "It is finished" (Jn 19: 30); earlier He had proclaimed: "'But I, when I am lifted up from the earth, will draw all men to myself.' He said this to show the kind of death he was going to die" (Jn 12: 32–33).

The Christ of the Grünewald reredos recalls a theatrical production of dramatic intensity, where the emotional dominates. Limp and succumbing from the weight of His wounded flesh, His body is even portrayed in a color of decomposition!

Let us return now to iconography, which prefers not to resort to the emotional, but to the spirit or rational instead, and emphasizes the *kenosis* —the abasement—of the God-man whose physical purity evokes, even compels, incorruptibility.

It is important that we try to understand how much representations of Christ "à la Grünewald," unfortunately so numerous in the West, often

31. *Crucifixion of Christ.* Mathias Grünewald, 16th c.
Detail of the Altarpiece of lsenheim, Unterlinden Museum, Colmar, France.
(Photo: O. Zimmerman)

32. *Crucifixion of Christ.* 17th c.
Semetkovic, Czechoslovakia.
(Photo: Michel and Lieselotte Quenot)

correspond to a public taste which has been conditioned over the centuries. They obliterate the divine dimension involved at the crucifixion.

In such religious art, the humanity of Christ overshadows His Divinity. Only disappointment and despair are perceived, without any indication of a victory or a resurrection, thus depriving the Holy Cross of its strength of Life. Admittedly, it is not necessary to be a Christian to bring human suffering into evidence; but you must indeed be a Christian to be able to "see" and "show," in Christ crucified, the glorious Christ of the Resurrection.

In his famous novel *The Idiot*, Dostoevsky has Mishkin exclaim: "Why, that's a painting that might make some people lose their faith!" Mishkin says this because he is profoundly upset, seeing a copy of the painting by Hans Holbein which depicts the cadaver of Christ with glazed eyes.

4. General facts about the icon

Preparation and materials

Windows on the Kingdom, icons are the fruit of long work requiring patience, experience and talent. The materials used for making an icon are respected as God created them to be used from the mineral, plant or organic world. They too are called to participate in the transfiguration of the cosmos, since the task of the iconographer is to spiritualize even our tangible reality.

The board, called "the support," serves as the base of the icon and requires for itself alone a long and tedious preparation. The painting depends on a well-prepared board to help preserve it from atmospheric conditions that may often vary considerably. Choice of wood for the board is particularly important: solid and well-aged wood is essential. Braces made of hardwood are used on the back to reinforce the board against warping. The central part of the board, destined to receive the drawing and picture of the icon, is often hollowed out about 1/8" deep, leaving a frame of 3/4" to 2" or more wide around the edge. The slight hollowing out of the board's surface, more frequent in Russian tradition than Byzantine, is called "kovcheg" in Slavonic. This term, used to designate reliquary cases or coffers for sacred objects, reminds us that the primary reason for the border around the icon is not so much to frame it, but to protect the holy image as if it were in a jewel case.

Painting techniques for the icon followed from the very beginning two artistic procedures developed in ancient times: the first is called "encaustic" (molten wax), which was progressively abandoned from the eighth century, i.e., toward the end of the iconoclastic crisis; the second is called "egg tempera" or simply "tempera." Today the egg tempera procedure is unfortunately being replaced more and more by modern commercial art materials—such as acrylics—which cannot truly equal tempera painting.

A coat of rabbit skin glue is brushed on to fortify the board which has previously been scored. It is then covered with a piece of thin canvas or cloth which has been soaked in the glue before spreading it onto the board; the cloth covering helps the gesso ground to stick better. It aids in preventing serious cracking of the colors and painting on the gesso surface caused by a possible warping of the wood beneath it. Use of a cloth covering was practically unknown until the end of the fourteenth century; it is rarely found on small Greek icons or on icons whose board was made from a very hard wood.

The glued cloth or just the board itself is covered with up to seven or more coats of a mixture called "levkas" in Russian, a mixture made with the rabbit skin glue and an extra-fine gesso powder like chalk or alabaster. This gesso ground dries hard and must then be polished perfectly smooth; onto this ivory-smooth surface the icon picture is drawn and lightly etched. Its design is inspired from either an iconographic manual or a reproduction of an ancient icon. Fidelity to iconic Tradition, a guarantee of authenticity, requires this practice, which in turn orients the creativity of the painter.

The gilding process follows. The background of an icon is in fact called its "light." Either yellow or red ochres are used, and sometimes a white varnish. Quite often the entire background is covered with genuine gold leaf; this complex procedure is mastered only with practice. Once the gilding has dried, the icon drawing is then covered with a coat of egg yolk emulsion, followed by the various basic color tone layers. The contours are accentuated and completed by the necessary highlightings which enliven the entire icon, thus spiritualizing matter. If the icon is not signed, despite the many infractions of this rule, it always receives a name linking it to its prototype.

Before being exposed to candle soot and dust, the icon is usually impregnated with a varnish of heated linseed oil, "olifa," to which is added some amber, resin or cobalt acetate. This varnish has the property of penetrating through the different layers of colors to improve their adhesiveness and enliven their brilliance. The attempts to replace it by using modern polyurethane varnishes have not always given complete satisfaction.

It is essential that the icon be able to resist the ordeals and wear of time, as it is a reflection of the incorruptibility of a new creation resurrected with Christ from the tomb on Easter morning.

The inscription of the name

It is by the inscription that the icon receives *a presence.* The strength of a name is recognized by all of the theistic religions, notably Islam, and in numerous ancient cultures, e.g., in Egypt, China and the Jewish world.

The ancient Egyptians maintained that the name was an integral part of the person himself. To write it or pronounce it made the person live on or prolonged his life. For the Chinese, to name an object or a person amounted to having an influence over them. The Hebrews attributed energies beyond all understanding to the name of Yahweh (YHWH = "I am Who I am," Ex 3:14), which only the High Priest could pronounce. God is present and active in His name, which conveys His power and blessing.

A detail we should note here is the beginning of a theology of the name of Christ outlined within the text of the *Shepherd of Hermas,* written towards the middle of the second century: "The name of the Son is great and immense, and it is He who sustains the whole world."

The name of Christ is inherent to His Person; it actualizes His active presence which we are unable to see. His name proves to be a powerful weapon against both evil and the Evil One. The inscription of His name confers on the icon its sacred character, its spiritual dimension.

Icons of Christ and of the Theotokos bear the Greek abbreviations for Jesus-Christ (IC XC = ʾIησοῦς Χριστός) and for the Mother of God (MP ΘY = Μήτηρ Θεοῦ). Depending on the origin of the icon, other inscriptions may often be added in a different language according to local

33. *Nativity of Christ.* Botticelli (1444–1510).
National Gallery, London, England.
(Photo: André Held)

customs. An iconographer's manual from Mt Athos proposes a series of different names or titles for Christ: "The All-Powerful," "Source of Life," "Savior of the World," "The All-Merciful," "Emmanuel," "The King of Glory," etc. Likewise for the Mother of God: "She who shows the way" (*Hodigitria*), "The Queen of Angels," "The Virgin of Tenderness" (Vladimir), "The Joy of All," "Comforter of the Afflicted," etc. We should also note that the nimbus or halo of Christ must bear the inscription ὁ ὤν: "He who is." It is written in the Cross of the halo either starting from the top, or from the left side around the halo, as can be seen in different variants.

The absence of naturalism

If the iconographer effaces himself by not signing his work, it is because in the icon there is more than the usual exclusive triangle found in all profane art: viz., the artist, his creation and the spectator. The icon is theophanic, a visible sign of the invisible presence; therefore it eclipses both the painter and the spectator by the very fact of its transcendent element, the sacramental presence. The characteristic absence of realism within authentic iconography serves to emphasize the spiritualization which is taking place. It goes without saying that what is purely "spiritual" cannot be drawn. To try to visualize or portray it by means of the "tangible" would be only to destroy it and contradict it. If images appeal to our senses, seeking to inspire within us a natural feeling, we must still insist on the fact that the icon is meant to be neither "touching" nor sentimental. The faces in iconic art are meant to be as much as possible faithful portraits, while representations of the land, the vegetable and animal worlds follow their own formal language. Both vegetable and animal worlds are often represented by allusions that contradict all natural logic; thus odd forms are often seen pictured in iconography. Perhaps if they are incomprehensible for us today, we should trust that someday we shall grasp the essentials, because we ought to have confidence in that manifest wisdom of the ancient iconographers.

Our corruptible and tainted world already participates with the icon in the deification of humanity and is consequently transfigured by it. Do we not have the example of saints speaking to wild animals, taming them, as Adam did before the Fall? This is an allusion to our future encounter with the mystery of Paradise! The icon, then, does not limit itself to being only represen-

34. *Nativity of Christ.* 16th c.
Transfiguration Monastery, Meteora, Greece.
(Photo: André Held)

35. *Nativity of Christ.* 20th c. by Monk Gregory Kroug.
(Photo: Andrew Tregubov)

tational or non-representational art; rather, it reveals to our mundane, unspiritual eyes the invisible, spiritual existence of the world beyond. And neither can we say that the icon is another form of abstract art. Far from it! The icon, after all, is based on the Incarnation of Christ. In fact, it would be correct to say that His Nativity also marks the birth of the icon. The icon can become figurative or representational whenever it represents for us again the life and features of a saint, but even when it does this, it is the spiritual dimension which emerges first and foremost; each graphic narrative in such icons is kept to a minimum. It is the interior, spiritual beauty of the icon which is more important than anything else, and not just the pure aesthetics of its art.

Leonid Ouspensky points out correctly "that the task of the icon is to guide every emotion as well as our reason and all the other faculties of our nature towards Transfiguration by eliminating any exaggerated elation which could be either unhealthy or harmful." At the same time as it portrays our deification, there is nothing human which remains foreign to the icon; it excludes neither the psychological aspect nor those features proper to man in his earthly environment.

If a person portrayed on an icon bears a certain resemblance to its prototype and is therefore depicted with the same style of clothing as when alive, the represented image has nothing carnal or corruptible about it, despite what can unfortunately be seen in those decadent icons influenced by Renaissance painting. Our corruptible body is replaced by a transfigured body filled with Divine Energies.

What, then, is the source of that malaise which so many people experience when they look at an icon? There is both attraction and a repulsion! One reason for this might be that the icon announces the joy of the Kingdom to the world, yet its message of asceticism projects a touch of sadness. This contrast between joy and sadness refers to the very essence of Christianity, where light unquestionably conquers darkness and suffering. The joys of Easter cannot be had without the sufferings of the Passion; Christ then triumphs by his Resurrection.

The icon questions us, but it will "speak" to us only after we have turned our backs on the reign of the flesh, to accept the Holy Spirit who alone can flood us with perfect joy.

Architecture

Drawn in defiance of human logic, architecture in iconography creates an evident denial of all constructional functionality. Correct proportions are not only completely ignored, but they do not correspond at all to the height of human figures pictured in the icon. The same is true of doors and windows, which are drawn strangely with whimsical measurements. A curtain draped between buildings suffices to symbolize that the scene is taking place inside. The laws of gravity have no place at all in this world. Is not the icon similar to the Gospels: a challenge to the wisdom and rules of this world? From this very reality are derived those forms which often seem so unusual and astonishing for us today.

There is no place here for any misunderstanding. The icon repudiates all pretenses because it manifests the heart or essence of every creature and the meaning of life. People of importance are indicated by name on the icon.

Let us add that if architectural forms, mountains and vegetation which compose the background are always of less importance than the people in the foreground, the different background elements are nonetheless integrated with the foreground and do not constitute an independent element of themselves. The icon of the Baptism of Christ gives us a fine example of such integrated harmony with its mountains on the right and the left. The icon of the Crucifixion also illustrates this quite well, with its walls of Jerusalem recessed in the background.

The Face

We have already pointed out that as a result of the Incarnation, the image of mankind assumes a new dimension. The will to spiritualize the world includes a transfiguration of the tangible world, where physical beauty is no longer important. While the beauty of the human body takes precedence by its naturalistic aspects in both Hellenic and Renaissance art, bodies often disappear in the icon beneath garments resembling Roman togas. These cloaks no longer drape physical bodies, but bodies and souls which are transfigured so that they glimmer with translucent light and colors. The folds of their clothing do not only express their physical movement, but rather the spiritual movement of the entire person. And this is so true that it almost becomes possible to discern the spiritual state of the Russian people over the centuries through the evolution of the folds in the clothing of their iconography.

36. *Saint Nicholas.* Russian, 16th c.
Castle de Wijenburgh, Echteld, Netherlands.
(Photo: St Vladimir's Seminary Press S–227)

If it should happen that the body be nude, as in the icon of the Baptism of Christ, its lack of naturalism only contributes to render it more spiritual in appearance. Such nudity does not at all "expose" the human body, since the icon's goal is not, as in secular art, to give prominence to natural physical beauty. The icon seeks to express visually theological truths and to incarnate a spiritual presence.

As the visual center of the body, the face dominates everything else. In his *Notes of an icon painter*, which we have already mentioned, Monk Gregory writes:

Only a picture that has a face looking at us and a human face transfigured by divine grace has the right to be a holy icon.

And further on he states:

The eagle which holds the Gospel Book cannot be the icon or image of John the Evangelist, but only his symbol.

Let us note here that the ancient Greeks called a slave *aprosopos*, i.e., he who has no face. So by assuming the features of a human face, God restored to us a face in His own image, chained as we were like slaves without faces—*aprosopos*—because of sin.

If Christian art from the beginning of Christianity gave us figures with full frontal views, the same was not true later on, without speaking of today, when real faces simply tend to disappear or just turn up as caricatures.

This is exactly what the renowned art critic René Huyghe declares in his book: *L'art et l'âme—Art and the soul*:

As fast as the human face, above all in its nobility, has disappeared from contemporary art works, its opposite—the Beast—has substituted itself in a strange way, appearing frequently as if to witness to a tacit obsession of our times. (Paris: Flammarion, 1980, p. 342)

Does not today's art reflect a world in crisis, deprived of security and truth? Despite a profusion without precedent of media at his disposal, modern man experiences a growing difficulty to meet or encounter his neighbor, whose face he so often does not even notice.

In iconography, only people who have not attained holiness are seen in profile. For instance, look at the Wise Men and the shepherds in the icon of the Nativity! This can point out for us the importance of frontality, which is already "presence." Direct contact demands it, as our experience in human relations only serves to confirm. A profile diverts this direct contact to a certain extent and depersonalizes the relation. So despite the suggestive impact of the subject, *The Kiss of Judas* by Giotto, showing Christ in profile, reveals something of an absence. In certain cases one should even speak of domination: the "you" of a face-to-face surrenders to the "he" that characterizes a person seen in profile.

By their frontality, figures in the icon attract the spectator, and open to him their inner life.

Nothing is more normal, since it is the head which determines the volume of the body and its position. The overall aspect of the body's anatomy is subordinated to the head. While the classical canon for physical beauty gives the proportion of five heads for the length of the body, it is accorded up to ten heads in iconography.

Faces seen in icons often have a rather dark, almost earth-like, color. Certainly, the face of Christ the New Adam, from the Hebrew *adamah*, meaning earth, belongs to a specific historical person. This in no way prevents the Holy Face of Jesus from belonging to all of humanity, which it recapitulates. Figures in ancient icons stare at eternity with their large eyes, very often opened in an exaggerated manner. This staring, intensified by the bold orbit of their eyes, fascinates the spectator.

An evolution in the representation of Christ can be noticed after the iconoclastic period, manifesting itself in a greater balance between the human and the divine. Influenced by the revival of the hesychast[1] tradition at Byzantium in the fourteenth century, and with even greater fervor in Russia in the sixteenth, the face of Christ became warmer, less severe.

1.Hesychasm, from the Greek word *hesychia*, tradition at Byzantium in the fourteenth century, meaning calm, solitude, interior peace, refers to the mystical prayer called *The Prayer of Jesus*, where communion with God is obtained by making our intellect descend into our heart with a constant repetition of the name of Jesus Christ associated with the prayer of the Publican (Lk 18:14)—"Lord Jesus Christ, have mercy upon me a sinner." Purified, our thoughts become attached to the memory of the Son of God and our heart opens itself to the action of the Holy Spirit. The term "hesychast" refers above all to the practice of that prayer which, although widespread during the first centuries of Christianity, had a new revival among the solitaries (hesychasts) of Mt Athos in the fourteenth and fifteenth centuries. Saint Gregory Palamas was its eminent defender and spokesman. Intimately bound to a spirituality of unsuspected richness, hesychasm penetrated into Russia and was developed notably at the famous monastery of the Holy Trinity–Saint Sergius. For a deeper spiritual understanding of hesychasm and the Prayer of Jesus one should perhaps read first *The Orthodox Way* by Kallistos Ware (St Vladimir's Seminary Press) and the excellent collection of *The Philokalia* in five volumes translated by G. Palmer, P. Sherrard and Kallistos Ware (Faber and Faber).

37. *The Kiss of Judas* (detail). Giotto, ca. 1305.
Scrovegni Chapel, Padua, Italy.
(Photo: Michel and Lieselotte Quenot)

38. *Saint Clement of Ohrid.* 14th–15th c.
National Museum, Ohrid, Yugoslavia.
(Photo: André Held)

Touched and sanctified by Divine grace, every organ of our senses has ceased to be the usual sensory organ of a biological man. The eyes are both animated and large, witnessing to the scripture verse of Ps 25:15, "My eyes gaze continually at the Lord," "because my eyes have seen Thy salvation" (Lk 2:30). They have been opened to marvel at the sublime and at the vision of the works of our Creator.

Looking at the rest of the face we see the forehead, the nose, the ears, the mouth and also the cheeks, which are given deep wrinkles for ascetics, monks and bishops. The forehead is often rather convex and quite high, expressing both the power of the Spirit and of wisdom, which are inseparable from love. The nose is thin and elongated, giving a nobility to the face. It no longer detects the scents of this world, but only the sweet odor of Christ and the life-giving breath of the Spirit gushing from a throat and neck which are disproportionately large. The mouth, being an extremely sensual organ, is always drawn finely and geometrically, eliminating its sensuality. The lips remain closed, because true contemplation demands silence. As a sign of spirituality, according to Cyril of Jerusalem (†387) the small mouth stresses that "the body no longer needs earthly nourishment because it has become a spiritual wonder" (Migne, PG 33, 613, *Catechesis* 18).

The ears, created to hear the commandments of the Lord, have become interiorized, and they no longer hear or listen to the sounds of this world. They are attentive only to the interior voice. An energetic chin can be noticed beneath an often bushy beard. Yet certain details are at times surprising: for instance, lusterless eyes, deformed or funny looking ears. This absence of naturalism, which is a non-conformity to nature as we see it, only reminds us that these transfigured bodies already perceive more, and even something else, than the majority of us do: they see the spiritual and not just the physical world. This abandonment of the naturalistic in portraying our sensual organs emphasizes a detachment from mundane excitements, a sort of deafness to worldliness in order better to grasp the spiritual world. Indeed, the Fathers of the Church see our senses as being the doors of our soul. And the father of monasticism, Saint Anthony the Great (born about 250 AD), insists upon how much the disorganized coming and going of images conveyed by our sight, hearing, touch, taste, smell and words, tarnishes the purity of our hearts.

39. *Nativity of Christ.* Moscow, 15th c.
(Photo: St Vladimir's Seminary Press S–309)

40. *The Protection of the Mother of God.* Russian, late 15th c., Novgorod School.
Compliments of the Temple Gallery, London.
(Photo: St Vladimir's Seminary Press S–348)

We grasp better now why these figures, whose forms are often hieratic, and the sober lines of the entire composition, do not provoke sentimentality but lead us to gaze and look toward the interior—the essence of life. In spite of their immobility, their bodies are never static; a spellbound appearance only better accentuates the dynamism of an interior life revealed by their ardent and confident eyes.

They are the image of flesh and blood obedient to the Spirit, according to the words of Holy Scripture: "Let all mankind be silent before the Lord" (Zech 2:17), so that the Almighty may manifest Himself.

If immobility expresses peace in God and suprahuman life, movement manifests here a lack of spiritual life, even the sinful state of humanity. This can be seen in the icon of the Transfiguration where, respectively on the left and right of Christ, Moses and Elijah are immobile, while the Apostles, frightened by the voice from heaven, betray confusion and agitation.

Lengthy fingers and elongated bodies indicate dematerialization in the most eloquent way, revealing the flow of spiritual intensity flooding forth from those who are portrayed on the icons.

The gold nimbus or halo around the head symbolizes the brilliance of Divine Light in the person who lives in the intimacy of God. The icon is more interested in the soul than in the body; it seeks to show the effect of the Holy Spirit on humanity, as manifested concretely by a resemblance with the Divine. This presence of the Holy Spirit is reflected above all in a person's face, as was witnessed by Nicholas Motovilov, who saw his spiritual father, Seraphim of Sarov, transfigured before him. Penetrated by Divine Light, the elder became "all face," as transparent as a rose petal before the flame of a candle.

Then Father Seraphim took me by the shoulders and holding them strongly he said:

"Both of us—you and I—are in the fullness of the Holy Spirit. Why do you not look at me?"

"I cannot look at you Father. A lightning flashes forth from your eyes that hurts mine. Your face is brighter for me than the sun itself."

Further on Motovilov continues:

Picture to yourself the face of a man who is speaking to you from the middle of the sun at its midday brightest. You can see the movements of his lips and the changing expressions of his eyes; you hear his voice and you feel his hands on your shoulders, but you can neither see his hands, his body, nor your own, but only a blinding light shining for many yards all around you, brightly illuminating the snow which covered the meadow and was falling on the great elder and on myself.

The evangelist Matthew already proclaims the true meaning of the halo: "Then the righteous will shine like the sun in the Kingdom of their Father" (Mt 13:43).

Just one more word here about the icons of Christ. Indisputably, the human face of the God-man remains inexhaustible, infinite in its beauty. Yet each iconographer stresses a distinguishing characteristic trait of this beauty in the quest to express a maximum harmony.

Time and place

The innovations of modern art are reduced to insignificance when compared to the audacity of iconographers who are "prisoners"—so to speak—of strict Canons, which in fact liberate since they permit a concentration of effort on the essentials. Iconography ignores the well-known relationship between time and space. A complete freedom reigns here, and iconographers do not hesitate to use it. All times and places can meet together. A fixed date or a particular place have no absolute value in this art, and the icon of the Nativity gives us a perfect example of this fact. The Nativity includes all the other great feasts and recalls for us every great event in the life of Jesus. The icon is intimately united here with the liturgy, which speaks of both the Pascha of the Nativity and the Pascha of the Resurrection.

Let us point out that the scene painted on this icon occurs in front of the grotto, never inside, for the grotto is pictured as being the deepest part of the background. In this way the iconographer stresses how the event itself extends beyond the actual historical spot, just as it is prolonged and perpetuated in time well beyond the moment of its realization.

Geometric structure and composition

Both order and peace inundate the icon, which offers us a vision of the world to come. Men and animals, landscapes and architecture, all participate in the divine harmony. Yet the harmony found in icons, which anyone can discern without being a subtle connoisseur of art, results from a well-defined structure. It is the fruit of a long tradition coupled with

41. *The Holy Trinity* of Rublev.
(Photo with the geometric lines)

42. *The Annunciation.* Church of St Clement of Ohrid, early 14th c.
Macedonia, Yugoslavia.
(Photo: St Vladmir's SeminaryPress S–318)

43. *Resurrection of Lazarus.* 12th–13th c.
Private collection, Athens.
(Photo: Michel and Lieselotte Quenot)

patient work seeking perfection. Without entering here into too many details, let us say that anyone who paints icons cannot risk an ignorance of geometry. This is true primarily because of the knowledge required for proportions and measurements, even though iconographers today do have at their disposal both sketchbooks and detailed manuals to help them. "Once again let us consider together the splendid fifteenth-century icon of the Nativity from the Rublev atelier. What do we see?" Different scenes belonging to distinct periods and places. Dividing this icon into three equal parts on the horizontal plane permits us to distinguish three levels or rows of interpretation: viz., at the top, the prophetic row; in the middle that of the Mystery itself; and on the bottom row, the human aspect. By dividing the surface of the icon again into nine equal rectangles forming a "grid," we can better elaborate our analysis. Each row is composed of three scenes. Reading from left to right in the top row we see the Wise Men, the star with its three rays symbolic of the Holy Trinity, and the angels, "messengers." In the middle are the angels in adoration, the Christ-Child with His Mother, and the shepherds. In the bottom row we find St Joseph beset with doubts, confronted by an old humpbacked shepherd; next, the cosmos symbolized by rocks, plants and earth; then finally we see the midwives busy with the work to be done at every birth. A deeper study would accomplish an even more refined appreciation of this icon. Readers with a sense of geometry should compare the position of the Christ-Child's head, first in relation to the entire composition and then to the head of the Theotokos; then draw a circle whose center is in the head of the Christ-Child…

The same circular structure is found in Rublev's masterpiece, the celebrated icon of the Holy Trinity (1411). Numerous studies written about it will enlighten the interested reader, but we nonetheless wanted to mention its example and importance.

Finally, one can notice that an invisible cross is generally present in the geometric structure, especially among the festal icons. Figures are also disposed in a symmetrical manner, so that there is always a central point of convergence which is either Christ or the Virgin.

The size of human figures

If mathematical relations between different parts of the body played a fundamental role in art for the ancient Greeks, Byzantine art evolved towards an abandonment of the three-dimensional aspect. The image of the new man regenerated by Christ refers to a world where dimensions no longer exist. It therefore produces an absolute freedom. The size of a person is usually determined by his or her importance and significance. The positioning of the person also becomes a factor; for instance, a person standing in the background can be larger than the person in the foreground. But even here the terms "foreground" and "background" misrepresent reality, since depth as such does not really exist and everything takes place in the forefront.

Perspective

This refusal of depth is illustrated and demonstrated very well by figures which generally stand out against a plain gold-leaf background, with neither decoration nor background scenery. Viewed in such a way outside of either time or space, they command our attention by their spiritual presence.

Perspective is most often ignored due to the fact that it simply imitates nature by employing pure technique. When used, iconic perspective is frequently "reversed." The vanishing point of reversed perspective is not situated behind the picture but rather in front of it. It cannot be found within the picture because it converges in front of the icon, toward the viewer. This means that the focus point actually moves out away from the icon toward the beholder, and the icon figures come forth to "meet" him. The result is an opening, a radiating forth, while the vanishing point in ordinary painting results in a convergence that closes up. In those icons whose subjects consist of people grouped together, depth is simply suggested by the overlapping of either heads or haloes of the group.

By using inverse perspective, iconography has embraced the entire concept of those Gospel teachings like the Sermon on the Mount, which completely reverse our secular, earthly values. And this also reminds us that it is God who takes the initiative to come forth and encounter humanity.

Light

All Byzantine art tends toward a transcending of forms that express the material or tangible. The mosaics of Ravenna are a hymn to light by the very beauty of their colors alone. Truly, light is *the* theme of iconography.

And yet an icon could never be brightened any more than you would try to brighten the sun. Wreathed and transfigured by Divine Light, the icon does not use shadows in its art.

We shall develop the theological implications of this theme later on in the book.

The importance of colors

Born from light, colors give both heart and soul to art forms. The great specialist and contemporary painter Johannes Itten states:

> I know that the deepest secret and the most essential action of colors remain invisible to the eye and can be contemplated only by the heart. The essential escapes every artistic method.

And elsewhere he says:

> Colors are radiating forces generating energies which have either a positive or a negative effect on us, whether we realize it or not. The ancient masters of stained glass used colors to create a mystic, supraterrestrial atmosphere within cathedrals and churches to help the faithful transport their meditation into the spiritual world.

The same fact is true for icon painters, but it involves even more than that. The ancients already thought that vision or sight transforms, and if this is true, we can indeed guess the consequences for the icon. Color speaks primarily to our sensibility, while the drawing speaks to our reason. Color also has a "significance"; its importance is mostly symbolic, even if the interpretations vary. On the religious level, the play of light and darkness symbolizes an ascensional force.

Christian art provides numerous examples of the use of colors as symbols: red for love and for the Holy Spirit, white for the Father, for faith, for purity, and so on. The seven colors of the rainbow permit the eye to perceive over 700 different shades of color. Is it necessary then to insist on why the use of color in icons requires a thorough knowledge of the subject such as the master iconographer possesses?

Much more than a decorative element, color plays a capital role in Byzantine iconography. Like language, the icon has its own way of expressing the transcendent world. By the relationships between its colors, icons can translate, beyond the reality of the picture itself, a profoundly spiritual message sensed by the subconscious. Even though it often origi-

nates from iconographic Tradition, the choice of a color conforms in a
great measure to the symbolic meaning. This of course limits the artist
who is no longer free to paint according to his personal whims; the
usefulness of the Canons previously mentioned is already evident. Yet it is
undeniable that color variations, which are an established fact, prove to us
that the choice of color often occurred during the actual work itself.
Iconographers forego using any of the classic repertory of optical illusion
such as chiaroscuro or shadowing, for those same reasons we have already
stated. Never drab nor somber, icon colors are striking both by their
brightness and liveliness. Horses and rocks painted in red ochre and pinks
only emphasize the refusal of realism, thus opening the pathway toward
spiritualization. These colors are mystical colors.

Starting with a dark base color, the iconographer obtains increasingly
lighter tones toward the final highlighting by painting with a procedure
called scumbling. On the clothing, particularly that of Christ in glory, the
Child-God, His Mother and also on the wings of angels, we frequently see
fine golden lines applied by a procedure called "hatching." The result is an
effect of shining light and joy; this procedure, also known as "assist," is
very important.

Gold, by the fact of its value as pure light, unlike colors which are only
refractions of pure light, symbolizes divinity—Light Itself—and an invisible
world which, as a metal in fusion, sparkles through transfigured bodies.

The chemical properties and tolerances of each color were understood
perfectly by the ancient Greek and Russian masters. Their colors were
either of mineral origin, carbonates, silicates, oxides, etc., or organic,
vegetable and animal substances, and have resisted the ravages of time. In
fact, while icons dating from the fifth century are well preserved, others,
often more recent and kept in more favorable conditions, can be found in
a deplorable state of deterioration. Among the various reasons for such
damage, the most apparent is without doubt ignorance. Another reason
might be the failure to observe those technical rules defined by experi-
enced and learned iconographers.

Perhaps we should mention the fact that colors became more important for the Russians than for the Greeks. Both geographic and climatic
surroundings, which contribute to fashioning the soul of a nation, are
certainly responsible for this, even if they do not explain everything.

Let us quote here the very beautiful text of the Russian philosopher Eugene Trubetskoy, written in 1916, whose words are still valid today:

The range of meanings is as infinite as the natural range of colors we see in the sky. First come the blues, of which the icon painter knows a great many—the dark blue of a starry night, the bright blue of day, and a multitude of light blues, turquoise, even greenish shades that pale toward sundown. We northerners often see these greenish blues after the sun has set. However, only the background is seen as blue; against it unfolds an infinity of the sky's other colors: the glitter of stars, the red of dawn, the reds of nocturnal storms or distant fires; and also the rainbow's many hues; and, finally, the gold of the midday sun.

In old Russian icons we find all these colors in their symbolic, otherworldly meaning. All are used by the artist to divide the empyrean from our terrestrial plane of being. This is the key to the ineffable beauty of the icon's color symbolism.

Apparently its guiding idea is this: the mysticism of icon painting is primarily solar, in that word's highest spiritual sense. However beautiful the sky's other colors may be, the gold of the midday sun remains the color of colors and miracle of miracles. All the others are, so to speak, of subordinate rank, forming a hierarchy around it. In its presence, the nocturnal blue disappears; the stars pale, and so does the glow from a fire at night. Even the red of dawn is merely a harbinger of sunrise. Finally, the play of sunrays produces every color of the rainbow, for the sun is the source of all color and all light in the sky and below it.

Such is the hierarchy of colors around the "sun that never sets." Not one color of the rainbow is denied a place in these images of divine glory, yet only the solar gold symbolizes the center of divine life. All the rest are its environment. Only God, "brighter than the sun," emits this royal light. The surrounding colors express the nature of the glorified celestial and earthly creatures that form his living, miraculously created Church. It is as if the icon painter by some mystic intuition had divined the secret of the solar spectrum discovered centuries later; as if he perceived all the blues of the rainbow as multicolored refractions of a single ray of divine life. (*Icons: Theology in Color*, by Eugene N. Trubetskoy. St Vladimir's Seminary Press, 1973, pp. 47–48)

The metal covering on the icon called the "riza" or "oklad," inherited from the sixteenth century, however beautiful it might be, often stemmed from an unconscious sense of iconoclasm. It simply deprives us of seeing the beauty of lines and colors conveying the world of the transcendent rendered present in the painted icon.

44. *The Last Judgment.* Moscow (?), 17th c.
The Louvre, Paris.
(Photo: André Held)

Colors and their meanings

Color for the physicist is a radiation having a certain wave length, as does light. So then it is not surprising that we are affected or transformed by its effects on us, as the ancients already believed. Color is present in the rhythm of the seasons—the colors of the leaves, the flowers, the fruits, etc.—so that we witness the colorful cycle of seasons varying between darkness and brightness. Three colors, blue, yellow and red, mixed with care, permit us to obtain all the colors modified as to their intensity, brightness and saturation.

Our eyes are intimately linked to our other senses and can perceive tones which are warm or cool, and colors which are rough or velvety, dry, soft or faded, not to mention all their different tones. Not only do our bodies react to color, but even more our souls, without our being able to provide exhaustive explanations. The psychological impact of color increases according to a person's cultural level. Psychiatry has used color as one of its tools for a long time. People suffering from depression are given a room painted red, while nervous people are given surroundings tinted blue or purple. The cool colors, shades of blues and greens, express and suggest calm, softness, tranquility, contemplation, sadness—the contrary of excitement; whereas joy, strength, force, activity and ardor are attributed to the warm shades of reds and yellows. Experiments in this field carried out in different factories have clearly confirmed the influence of colors on the performance and output of workers. Even animals are not exempt from the influence of colors. Red can provoke roosters, dogs and certain insects. And since we shall comment on each color separately, let us note that a black package seems heavier than a white one; a red room warmer that a blue room; telephone conversations last much longer in a blue phone booth than in a red one. As for the old expression "to be in a black mood," it only confirms the effect that black can have on us from a psychological point of view.

Should we be surprised then at the interest among the Byzantines in using colors as well as possible in their sacred art?

White: The opposite of black, white is not strictly speaking a color, but sums up all the colors, if they are to be considered colors originating from light. Indeed, nothing is more luminous than white light. It is therefore only normal that white symbolizes light which has the property of diffusing itself and flashing through space. A symbol of the eternal, white belonged to the gods of earliest antiquity. The Tibetan word *hot-tkar* means "white and One," a reference to the unity of God. Virgil describes the god Pan—meaning "All"—who was the principle of life, as being "white as snow" (*Georgics* III, verse 391). Celtic priests or druids were clothed in white. The ancient Egyptians thought that white was joyful and sumptuous. They wrapped their dead in white linens because death separates light from darkness and the soul from the body. White is the color for mourning among native Africans, who also use it to avert and banish death.

Among the first Christians, baptism was called "illumination." The newly-baptized were vested in a robe of pure white as a sign of their birth to true life. White became the color of revelation, grace, and theophany.

Mountain tops imply a stronger light; are they not often a world of eternal snows reserved for the gods? God manifested Himself to Moses on Mount Sinai in a display of lightning, and the Lord was transfigured in blinding light on Mount Tabor. We find that same dazzling whiteness of Christ's robe in the Transfiguration icon and in numerous icons of the Resurrection, likewise in the famous frescoes of the Kariye Djami in Constantinople. White is the color of those who are penetrated by Divine Light: the angels at the Lord's tomb and of the Ascension, as well as the elders of the Apocalypse. Even the nimbus or halo of saints is often white—except when gold has been used instead. God the Father wears a white robe in the icon called the "Paternitas"—an icon condemned by the Council of Moscow, because God the Father was never incarnate, and is therefore invisible. Hierarchs of the Byzantine Church pictured on icons wear white liturgical vestments with contrasting black crosses as a double symbolism of the glory and passion of Christ.

But each color also has a certain ambivalence. According to experiences in psychoanalysis, the snowfield of a glacier recalls death, just as white horses seem to predict it. In the icon of the Nativity, the white of the New-Born against the black of the grotto, or that of Lazarus in the icon of his resurrection, also remind us of the tomb and death.

White is the color of purity: "Your sins will become as white as snow" (Is 1:18). It is the color of Divine Wisdom and of complete knowledge (great saints often have an unusual understanding); it likewise expresses joy and happiness. In his book *Du spirituel dans l'art et dans la peinture en particulier*, Kandinsky evokes its dynamism:

> White acts upon our souls like an absolute silence... This kind of silence is not at all a silence of death, for it overflows with living possibilities. (Paris: Denoël/Gonthier, 1979, p. 128)

Blue : Unquestionably, blue is the deepest, the most immaterial of all the colors—also the coolest. It offers a transparency proven by the limpidity of water, air and crystal, so that our gaze disappears into its depths.

Color of the heavens par excellence, blue is consequently predominant in medieval stained-glass; it reduces somewhat the material quality of the forms that it surrounds. It is passive on the material level because of its weak radiance; but it becomes eminently active on the spiritual level, oriented as it is towards the transcendent, and guides our spirit on the path of faith of which it is the chromatic symbol.

Blue also possesses a characteristic of interiorization and discretion, which suggests silent humility. Darker tones of blue accentuate its interior action as well as its attraction towards the infinite. If painted lighter, it seems to become distant and indifferent. We should note the fact that the contrast of a color tone with one or more different colors changes its chromatic value.

The above-mentioned transparency of blue makes it a natural ally of white. It was once a symbol of immortality among the Chinese and of truth for the Egyptians, whose high priest wore a blue sapphire and officiated in blue vestments, so we can deduce its link with the divine.

The encounter between heaven and earth puts the celestial colors of blue and white in opposition to the terrestrial colors of red and green. The popular icon of Saint George slaying the dragon gives us a fine example of such chromatic contrasts. In Greek mythology, the father of both men and gods is called Zeus, which means life, ether, the heavens, warmth and fire. His cloak, either an ethereal sky-blue or fire-red, conveys the closeness between wisdom and love in that supreme divinity.

Although highly valued in the Orient—above all in fabrics and in the superb Persian and Ottoman ceramics—blue was ignored in the New Testament, and it is rarely mentioned in the Old Testament. Here is mentioned only the blue-purple vestment worn by the High Priest (Ex 28:31) who communicated with God in the Tent of the Covenant, which was woven with a cloth of the same shade (Num 4:6–12).

Blue and white are attributed to the Virgin Mary, expressing detachment from this world and the soaring of the soul toward God. The icon of the Dormition—the feast of the Virgin Mary celebrated on August 15—painted by Theophanes the Greek, which can be contemplated at the Tretiakov Gallery in Moscow, offers a perfect example. The scene of the Dormition in the icon of the Deisis and the Great Feasts is directly inspired from it.

Dark blue is a sign of the mystery of Divine Life and dominates in iconography. It is the color of the mandorla centers in icons of the Transfiguration and of Christ in Glory. Blue is most often the color of the vestment of the Pantocrator, the robe of the Virgin and of the Apostles, not to mention the blues seen in Rublev's icon of the Trinity.

Red and purple : Being a limitless color, red is near enough to light that it is sometimes used as the background color for an icon. It reveals the dynamism of exuberant activity without imitating the dissipation of vivid yellow. Because of its forceful, irresistible radiance and its close link to the color of blood, principle of life, red is often considered as the first among the colors. Possessing a terrestrial character, it symbolizes youth, beauty, wealth, health, love, but also war. It is associated with all the great festivities among numerous and different nationalities.

If divine love—the Holy Spirit—is expressed symbolically by pure red, a reddish-orange frequently colors the flag of revolutionaries. To lose one's blood (red) amounts to losing one's life. Wine, a result of the sun, is the image of blood which rejoices the heart and accelerates its pulse. Plotinus in his *Enneades* (Book VI, ch. 3) sees fire as being one of the archetypes of beauty. The cipher for the Holy Trinity is the number 3, which is itself an image of fire since *vahni* in Sanskrit is translated both as fire and as three (love and communion). We celebrate the feast of St John the Baptist during the summer solstice when the sun is at its zenith; this feast announces Jesus Christ as He who will baptize no longer with water, but with fire (Mt 3:11). The Nativity of Christ is commemorated just at the time when daylight stops waning and the sun begins its ascent to prolong daytime once again. The icon of the Nativity reveals the "New Sun," the Light shining in the darkness of night.

A symbol of sacrifice and of altruism, red is an important color in Christianity. The tunic of Jesus in the praetorium is red, as are vestments for martyrs, the cloak of St Michael the Archangel and the fire-red Seraphim, whose name in Hebrew means "burning." But let us also note that red can similarly mean egoism, hatred, diabolical pride and by extension, hell-fire.

Purple was reserved for the highest of dignitaries by Homer himself in the *Odyssey* (XIX, 225). We also read in the Bible the passage of Daniel receiving purple robes as a reward (Dan 5:29), and in the parable of Lazarus, the rich man is dressed in purple (Lk 16:19). For the Byzantines purple was the symbol of supreme power. Their emperors always wore purple, except during their assistance at liturgical ceremonies, for which they dressed in white. Furthermore, Justinian's Code strictly forbade the sale and trading of purple dye or cloth outside Byzantium.

Red and blue, although strongly contrasted spiritually, create a good harmony. This fact is particularly noticeable as we look at the Virgin Theotokos dressed in a red maphorian, symbol of her humanity, and a blue robe, symbol of the divine, for she is the human creature who bore in her womb the Son of God. The purple robe and blue cloak of the central angel in the icon of the Trinity by Rublev emphasize at once the humanity, the sacrifice and divinity of Christ. The purple vestment is both royal and priestly. The two colors bear testimony to the two distinct natures assumed by Christ in a unique hypostasis.

Let us add here that in icons representing just one person, you can often see that when the cloak is of one color, the rest of the clothing is painted in a complementary color. The same is true in icons depicting scenes from the Gospels. Moreover, the colors are generally quite distinct from one another in such icons.

Green : It is the complementary color of red, something like water is to fire. Since it is a color that comes from the plant world and springtime, it symbolizes revival. The green of chlorophyll is produced by the light of the sun and is conditioned by the humidity of water. "Green" and "life" are two words that are closely connected, e.g., to have "green fingers," to be "green" with envy, or still "green" behind the ears!

Both the Greeks and the Romans dedicated green to Aphrodite and to Venus, goddess of love and beauty born from the sea. The Egyptians saw green as being the principal color of the plant world, of youth and of health, and they are seconded in this by Dionysius the Areopagite. All of the Mediterranean cultures, from the Old Testament to Islam, have attached great symbolic meaning to the color green.

Situated between the coolness of blues and the warmth of reds, a pure green is the perfect balance resulting from a mixture of blue and yellow, representing calm or absence of movement. As soon as you add some yellow or blue, a pure green changes, lending itself to extensive, varying mixtures.

As a symbol of spiritual regeneration, green is frequently the color of the prophets and of John the Evangelist, all of whom are heralds of the Holy Spirit. To have leafed through a book about icons only once is sufficient to realize how much green contributes to the painting of those it helps portray.

Yellow and gold : On the level of radiance, yellow should be considered like red, even though it is brighter; hence a relative similarity which is rather difficult to circumscribe. Although a pure yellow represents truth, a dull or pale yellow symbolizes pride, adultery, betrayal; all of them disagreeable odors of infernal brimstone, a synonym for sulphur, which is yellow.

Gold is far more interesting for our present study. Numerous ancient tribes were devoted to a solar cult. For the Egyptians, the sun itself, the gods, and pharaohs were believed to be made of gold. The golden Buddhas remind us of illumination; and in history, the expression "the Golden Age" stresses a particular era of perfection. Let us not forget that the gold seen on cupolas and in Byzantine mosaics symbolizes the world beyond, a world where the sun never sets.

Gold is unalterable, representing thus for Christians eternal life, faith and above all Christ Himself: Sun of Justice, Light of the World, Splendor of the rising sun. Yet even here we encounter ambivalence, because gold itself, while symbolic of the sun's radiance, can unfortunately also become symbolic of perversion and greed: a status symbol today in collections of gold jewelry and coins.

Again, gold is itself not a color seen in everyday nature, so that the golden background of the icon creates a "space" where bodies no longer need to conform to the elements of either scenery or architecture. Liberated from all that is terrestrial, they are spiritualized—transfigured in the golden light of eternity.

45. *Tikhvin Mother of God.* Novgorod, early 16th c.
Castle de Wijenburgh, Echteld, Netherlands.
(Photo: St. Vladimir's Seminary Press S–326)

If, in one way, the metallic reflection of gold imitates the shining sun and the brightness of candle flames, in another way it intensifies the different color tones in an icon by contrasts that result in a wondrous harmony.

The Hebrew word *aour*, meaning light, is similar to the Latin word *aurum*, meaning gold, which in India is considered a mineral of light. Also, the Latin noun *oratio*, meaning word, refers to the French word *or* meaning gold, and surprisingly enough, this French word is even used in the English language to designate the heraldic color *gold!* In fact, the ancient Greeks said of someone who excelled as an orator that he had a golden mouth. Gold symbolizes the divine light. If gold symbolizes light, we can see the consequences of this in the way gold is used in iconography, be it in the background or applied to persons or objects.

Brown : The color of earth, of clay and of sod, brown results from a mixture of red, blue, green and some black. It suggests dead leaves, autumn and the decomposition of plants, which turn into dark soil. An extensive palette of browns can be mixed by a gradual shading from the prime colors. Brown does not at all possess the dynamics and radiance of these latter. And yet icons are often painted in different tones of ochres, playing with light and conveying the image of a transfigured land celebrating the Paschal banquet.

The monastic habit, as a symbol of poverty and of humility, from the Latin word *humus* meaning earth or soil, recalls a slow death to the world, so that the monk may become a fertile "soil" for the grace of God; hence the clothing of monks is painted on icons with shades of brown or black.

Black : Like white, black is the absence of color, yet in reality black embodies all the colors together. Symbolically, white represents the unity of light, while black is its denial. Suggestive of non-existence, chaos, anxiety and death, black absorbs light without reflecting it. But the black of night promises the profusion of dawn. Holy Scripture sees in black the darkness and night that preceded the origins of creation: "Now the earth was a formless void, there was darkness over the deep" (Gen 1:2). The earth's dark abode of the dead contains the seed of rebirth and becomes fertile: "If the grain of wheat does not die…" According to the Swiss psychologist Carl Jung, black is a symbol of time and the site of germination. Thus it can be considered as a color of transition leading us to new life.

In icons the black habit of monks stresses their renunciation of the world's vanities, a prerequisite for the vision of Divine Light. Since life passes away without light, the damned are painted black in the icon of the Last Judgment; devils are also black or red, and sometimes brown. In the icon of the Nativity of Christ, the grotto is black. We see the same for the tomb of Lazarus, the grotto beneath the Cross, and Hades in the Paschal icon of the Descent to Hell.

These few considerations help us to recognize the vast field of research involved with colors and their use in iconography. If we seem to have stressed it within the framework of this limited study, it is simply due to the fundamental importance of the subject.

The thorough understanding of colors and their symbolism contributes greatly to the beauty seen in icons, which fascinates even the great masters of modern painting. A proof of this fact comes from the French painter Matisse, who was much enthused at the sight of icons during his trip through Russia toward the beginning of this century. And the great Swedish scientist Engström declared at the end of his long journey across Russia in 1923:

> Such harmony in colors has never been attained either before or since. We should send our painters to Russia, the young and the old, to learn a respect for spiritual balance—which is nothing else than the mystery of faith! Here in Russia I have celebrated a truly sublime festival of art. (from his book, *Muscovites*)

The bond between word and sight

A question comes to the fore as we conclude the present chapter: how much do we really understand about the impact of the visual on our hearing, and reciprocally, of hearing on our sight? The subject is of prime importance when we recall that in Orthodoxy, the Word of God in the Sacred Scriptures, our liturgical texts and icons, are all intimately linked together. How could we resist the message of the Gospel proclaiming the Nativity, as we contemplate simultaneously the icon of this great feast day? The Word of God has in the icon an irreplaceable support, because the icon offers a more vivid revelation of the mystery that the Word proclaims. The latter is thus assimilated in a special way by our sight, as we suggested earlier during our study of gold and its use in iconography. Modern science confirms that half of what we hear results from what we see. Furthermore, every sacred reading assumes a new dimension for the faithful who love and venerate icons, a dimension which we could call a "visual echo"!

46. *Myrrhbearing Women at the Tomb.* Russian, 16th c.
Castle de Wijenburgh, Echteld, Netherlands.
(Photo: St Vladimir's Seminary Press S–330)

3

Analysis of Several Icons

1. Icons of the Mother of God

After the icon of Christ, a constant reminder for us of His Incarnation, it is only natural that the icon of His Mother receives our veneration. Is she not the most beautiful jewel of all humanity, the ultimate example of the deification of mankind? Proclaimed as *Theotokos*—The Bearer of God— by the Council of Ephesus in 431 AD, she could only receive this name following the doctrinal definition that Christ her Son was both "true God and true man." The ubiquitous icons of the Virgin and Child, so loved, so prized by both iconographers and faithful, proclaim and confirm that same mystery. These icons are quite often venerated as patrons of a particular church or monastery, even of an entire nation.

The Orthodox Church always represents the Theotokos with her hair, upper forehead and shoulders hidden beneath a veil having a gold-fringed border. It is called the *maphorion*. The Virgin with hair exposed, as we so frequently see in the religious art of the Western Church, is simply unthinkable and inadmissible. Three golden stars decorate the maphorion, one above the forehead and one on each shoulder. Although these three stars are considered by some as a symbol of the Holy Trinity, iconographic Tradition has generally considered them as being symbolic of her virginity: before, during and after childbirth.

Orthodoxy distinguishes four major iconographic representations of the Mother of God:

1. The Mother of God Enthroned

2.   "   *Orans* (praying)

3. "She Who Shows the Way" (*Hodigitria*—from the Greek "odos," the way).

4. The Mother of God Merciful (*Eleousa*—from the Greek "eleos," mercy or pity)

From these four basic icon types, we count today over 230 variants. This fact alone gives us an idea how vast and rich iconography can be!

Let us point out some other descriptive epithets given to numerous icons of the Theotokos from early times: *Kardiotissa*—The Virgin of Tenderness; *Balikliotissa*—Source of Life; *Galactotrophusa*—the Virgin of the Blissful Womb.

In addition to its sacred function, the name of an icon of the Theotokos often refers to the place of its origin. The Russian cities of Vladimir, Iaroslav, Smolensk, Tver, Tikhvin, Korsun, Kazan, Novgorod, and others have lent their names to famous icons.

Combining the name of origin with that of the icon's function is also frequent, permitting a more precise definition; thus we speak of the Hodigitria-Vladimirskaia icon, or of the Hodigitria-Smolenskaia, of the Eleousa-Korsunskaia and so on.

- The classic model of the *Theotokos Enthroned* shows the Mother of God seated on a throne in a frontal position. She holds Christ on her lap, who blesses and presents a scroll of Scripture. On either side of the throne is an angel, or sometimes a saint, bowing towards the Child-God as a sign of adoration.

If the name *Platytera*—"She whose womb is more spacious than the heavens"—is often encountered, this name does not designate a specific type of icon, since it is frequently attributed to the "Virgin of the Sign," among others.

- The *Orans* is more often portrayed with the Child Jesus than without Him. In the first, where she receives as title "The Virgin of the Sign" (*Znamenie* in Russian and *Blachernitissa* in Greek), Christ is represented in a mandorla in front of the bosom of His Mother. Suspended mysteriously, He seems to escape the very laws of earth's gravity. God whom the entire universe could never contain is confined within the womb of the Virgin. The allusion to the words of the Prophet Isaiah could hardly be omitted here: "Therefore the Lord God Himself will give you a sign. It is this: the Virgin is with child and will soon give birth to a son whom She will call Emmanuel" (Is 7:14), which means "God with us."

The face of the Child is that of an adult with a large forehead full of wisdom; He holds a scroll containing the Scriptures and blesses with His

47. *Theotokos Enthroned.* Late 15th c. by Andreas Ritzos.
From the Monastery of St John the Theologian, Iraklion, Crete.
(Photo: Michel and Lieselotte Quenot)

48. *Theotokos 'Orans' called 'Virgin of the Sign'* (detail). 16th c.
Outside fresco, Moldovita monastery church, Bucovina, Romania.
(Photo: Michel and Lieselotte Quenot)

49. *Theotokos Eleousa.* 20th c. by Leonid Ouspensky (†1987).
Private collection, Paris.
(Photo: Michel and Lieselotte Quenot)

right hand. The Virgin raises Her arms in a gesture of prayer and of adoration.

The icon called the "Burning Bush" also belongs to this group.

- In the *Hodigitria* icon—"She who shows us the way"—the Theotokos looks majestically at the spectator and points with her right hand to the Child she carries on her left arm. He is dressed in robes dazzling with gold, to remind us of His divinity; He presents Himself as an adult always holding the Scripture scroll and blessing with His right hand. He is seen as *Emmanuel,* conscious of His role as Savior, in a frontal pose overflowing with grandeur and dignity.

This Hodigitria type holds a privileged place among icons since it is inspired directly from the first icon of the Virgin that was painted, according to Tradition, by St Luke himself. The iconographer's manual of Mount Athos states that icon painters should prostrate themselves before the Hodigitria and beseech Christ in prayer before they begin to paint.

- The *Eleousa* Virgin, called *Oumilenie* in Russian, means mercy, or also tenderness. The most prestigious and well-known example is the Virgin of Vladimir, a Byzantine icon introduced in Kievan Rus' in about the twelfth century. The relationship between the Mother and Child is expressed with a stunning force. Hugging her cheek to cheek, the Child seems to seek refuge near His Mother, who already foresees His passion. She embraces Him with her affectionate, maternal protection.

2. The icon of the Pantocrator and the Deisis

We may distinguish three major iconographic representations of Christ: the *Mandylion* or *acheiropoietos* icon offered to King Abgar; the *Emmanuel* or Child-God with adult features represented half-length in a gesture of blessing and holding the Scripture in His left hand; and the Pantocrator: the Almighty or Lord of the Universe. This latter is by far the most common of the three.

Present in the majority of Byzantine churches, the Pantocrator is painted in the highest place of honor within the church, the center of the principal dome. Among the vast number of frescoes and mosaics dedicated to this particular theme, the most poignant of all is without doubt the Pantocrator of Daphni near Athens, rendered in mosaic by an artist of the eleventh century. With His gaze plunging down on the faithful gathered below, this Christ-Pantocrator seems to scrutinize the very depths of their hearts. The facial expression seen here, quite severe and indeed peculiar to Byzantium, contrasts with a kinder, warmer expression in the Slavic icons.

According to iconographic canons, the Pantocrator is pictured either half-length or seated in majesty. He is often enthroned between celestial hierarchies in a manner that emphasizes His divine majesty. His gaze and gestures captivate His supplicants. The fingers of His right hand bless as do priests in the Byzantine tradition; this can be noticed by the very precise position of His fingers in the drawing. Both traditional versions presented here demonstrate this: we see the first two fingers joined and raised together recalling the two distinct natures of Christ, while the other two fingers joined to the thumb form three fingers symbolizing the Holy Trinity. Let us note in the second version that the fingers trace by their positioning the Greek monogram for Jesus-Christ (IC–XC) which is written on all of His icons, even in Russia.

His head is always surrounded by a nimbus bearing within it a Cross, which is usually inscribed with the Greek letter ὸ ὤν, meaning "I am Who I am" (Ex 3:14). The Pantocrator holds the Gospel book with His left hand; it is sometimes opened to a passage such as, "I am the Light of the world," or "He who follows Me walks not in darkness but in light," or "I am the Way, the Truth and the Life," etc. He wears a red robe or tunic called a *chiton*, covered with a dark blue or green cloak—royal colors reminding us of His two distinct natures.

Upon closer examination, one can distinguish two types of the Pantocrator in iconography. The first heightens and brings to the fore the cosmic significance of the Almighty "King of Kings and Lord of Lords" (1 Tim 6:15). The second type accentuates the redemptive work of Christ based on the Gospel inscription we mentioned above: "I am the Light of the world. He who follows Me walks not in darkness but will have the light of life" (Jn 8:12). This inscription is found on a majority of the Pantocrator icons.

Surely we must recognize that if an iconography of the Pantocrator draws on the visions of the Old Testament prophets—"The heavens are my throne and the earth is my footstool" (Is 66:1)—it also borrows primarily from the Ascension narrative given to us by the Evangelist Luke

50. and 51. Details from two icons showing both variants of the blessing hands of Christ.
(Photo: Michel and Lieselotte Quenot)

52. *The Mother of God (Virgin of Tenderness)*. 20th c. by Monk Gregory Kroug.
Montgeron, Paris.
(Photo: Andrew Tregubov)

(24:50–52), and from the Acts of the Apostles (1:9–11). To the stern Pantocrator of frescoes and icons portraying "He Who is" reigning unapproachable in the cosmos, the icons of the Ascension offer in contrast the solemn enthronement of Christ accompanied by two or four angels:

> As He said this He was lifted up while they looked on, and a cloud took Him from their sight. They were staring into the sky when suddenly two men in white were standing near them and they said, "Why are you men from Galilee standing here looking into the sky? Jesus who has been taken up from you into heaven, this same Jesus will come back in the same way as you have seen Him go there." (Acts 1:9–11)

Although the Pantocrator seen in iconography forms the upper section of the Ascension icon—a fact confirmed by art historians—the Ascension itself eludes all secular historical proof. If Pontius Pilate, whose existence is verified by historians, figures as a proof of the crucifixion of Christ, the Ascension tells us about Christ's taking His place at the right hand of the Father (Mk 16:19). Here we have to deal with a theological fact that evades historico-scientific critique, just as the Resurrection itself, about which we shall speak further on.

The icon of the Ascension is above all an eschatological icon (from the Greek word *eschaton*: that which concerns the final realities), because the angels of the Ascension announce that Jesus will return again in the same manner as He ascended into Heaven. The icon of the Pantocrator is thus an image of Christ seated at the right hand of the Father and still ever present, i.e., present to us from the time of His Ascension to that of the Parousia—the Second Coming of Christ. Our modest commentary only intimates the extremely rich content of this popular icon.

The Deisis icon—from the Greek word meaning *intercession*—is quite widespread, and cherished dearly by both the Greek and the Slavic peoples. It shows us the Pantocrator either in a half-length pose or seated on a throne, surrounded by saints who intercede on behalf of the faithful. In the smaller version of the Deisis, only the Theotokos and John the Forerunner surround the Christ Pantocrator. But in the larger composition of the Great Deisis, the twelve apostles and the two archangels are also included. Quite rarely the Theotokos and John the Baptist cede their place to a special patron saint, to a local saint or angels; however, Christ always remains the central figure.

53. *The Ascension.* Mid-16th c. From the iconostasis of the Church of the Transfiguration of the Savior at Nereditsa. Novgorod Museum.

As Forerunner of the Messiah, John the Baptist received the following tribute from Jesus Himself: "I tell you: of all the children born of women, there is no one greater than John. But the least in the Kingdom of God is greater than He is" (Lk 7:28). Though loftier than the prophets—and however great he is—John nonetheless remains a saint of the Old Testament. Yet all the saints of the Old Testament, with John at their head, have by virtue of Christ's Resurrection become mediators of the New Testament, and the Theotokos represents the most beautiful of its flowers.

The Deisis is an icon of the Wedding Feast of the Lamb: Christ is accompanied there by His bride, the Church, represented by the Theotokos. Friend of the Bridegroom (Jn 3:29), the Forerunner leads the Bride who is the Church, and it is for this reason that Orthodoxy bestows such privileged honor on the Baptist.

Byzantium also sporadically represents Christ as High Priest adorned with a royal crown bearing the inscription, "The King of Kings and the High Priest." The book He holds in His hand is opened, with one side bearing the inscription, "My Kingdom is not of this world," and the opposite side, "Take and eat, this is my Body given for the remission of the sins of the world." To the terrestrial *basileus* of Byzantium now corresponds the celestial *Basileus*.

3. The icon of the Crucifixion

Somewhat more practical than the Eastern Church, which is more contemplative, the Western Church, seeking to stimulate its faith, wants to touch, to see and to feel. Compared to the mystery of the Resurrection, the Crucifixion overwhelms us as a phenomenon. The Nicene Creed proclaims that Christ was "crucified under Pontius Pilate." It thus verifies the death of Christ, which any serious historian admits, and about which the Gospels testify amply. The Western Church is fascinated by the Cross and its sorrowful aspect, while Orthodoxy sees Jesus not as being abandoned on the Cross in his humanity, but filled with the glory of God. Our crosses do not always bear the well-known Greek abbreviated inscription, INBI—meaning "Jesus of Nazareth King of the Jews"—but sometimes instead: "The King of Glory and of the Angels"—an expression used by the Apostle Paul (1 Cor 2:8) and by St John Chrysostom: "I see Him

54. *Icon of the Deisis and some of the Great Feasts.*
Painted in 1984 by a Russian immigrant.
(Photo: Michel and Lieselotte Quenot)

crucified and I call Him King" (PG 49, 413). During the entire Paschal cycle, the liturgy continually chants, "…trampling down death by death…" (Paschal troparion), clearly emphasizing that the death of Christ on the Cross is not a failure but is already the victory over death. Hence the iconographer does not show us a tortured body that looks vanquished; he paints instead the Master of Life radiating the Divine Presence. The icon chosen here to illustrate this, is attributed to the renowned Russian, Master Dionysius, who was trained at the school of Rublev's successors. It was painted in about 1500 for the iconostasis of a monastery and figures among the most beautiful of Russian icons.

Very slender and sober, the long, thin cross occupies the center of the composition in perfect harmony. The body of Christ, considerably elongated and very graceful, leans slightly toward His Mother, who is comforted and supported by three women who mourn. Suffering with intense grief, yet without manifest tears, Mary leaves the group. Her right hand points toward her Son; she is interested only in His wounded body which seems freed from earth's gravitation to incline toward His Mother. Crucified with Her Son and in full communion with Him, she gives no consideration at all to rebellion, for she accepts the love of the Good Shepherd (Jn 10:11) who lays down His life for his sheep: "No one takes my life from me; I lay it down of my own free will" (Jn 10:18).

To the left of Christ is the beloved disciple John the Evangelist, absorbed in meditation. Behind him stands Longinus, the centurion, astonished and full of respect, but the light colors of his attire seem to efface his presence.

With tall, almost ethereal bodies, all of the figures in this icon help to reinforce the vertical aspect of the composition, the *descensus* and the *ascensus* of the Crucified, i.e., the descent to the realm of death and the rising to the Kingdom of Life. The third or lowest cross-piece seen beneath His feet represents the balance of destiny: the two opposing kingdoms which the Cross brings together just long enough to liberate the captives.

The Cross stands as a symbol having cosmic and universal meaning; it soars toward the four cardinal points. It was raised on Mount Golgotha, the sacred space considered in biblical tradition to be the center of the earth. Traditional societies' conception of the world considers mountain tops as being meeting places between heaven and earth.

"Tree of Life planted on Calvary" (from the Office of the Exaltation of the Cross—September 14th), the Cross is anchored in the center of the earth on the *omphalos* of the world—Greek meaning "navel"—the black cavern where Adam's skull is buried.

Planted thus in the heart of the world, the Cross is, figuratively speaking, the axis of our planet which connects the three cosmic levels: the firmament-heaven; our earth; and the lower world-hell, into which the Tree of Salvation plunges its roots.

If an embryo is attached to its mother by means of the umbilical cord which later forms the "navel," humanity also finds its vital principles in these two spiritual centers: Calvary and the Cross. Furthermore—and readers will surely have grasped this fact—Christ gives up His life at the very center of the Cross, revealing with an unbelievable force that our entire cosmos participates in the wondrous mystery of His Death and Resurrection. This is a message of unsuspected meaning, whose wealth these few lines only touch upon, but which would merit a thorough study of its own.

Let us return to the scene of the Crucifixion. The blood of the New Adam flows from His open side onto the skull of our first father, who thus re-inherits eternal life. Can we not recognize here the relationship between this icon and the icon of the Nativity? Christ is born in the very heart of darkness; our redemption takes place at the center of our world.

His eyes closed, Christ is truly dead. And yet, what feelings of peace, of communion and of dignity this icon conveys! His bowed head seems to portend a profound sleep. "Life has fallen asleep and hell shudders in terror" (from the office of Holy Saturday; sticheron from Lauds). Two angels, hovering above the Cross with their hands covered by their cloaks in the typical Byzantine sign of respect, call our attention to the divine sphere by their adoration. On the left, beneath the crossbeam, the outer angel pushes toward Christ a figure who personifies the Church. On the right, another angel drives away a figure with a woman's head, who personifies the Synagogue and glances back in an expression of anguish. In the background, the human sphere represented by figures of people, rise the walls of Jerusalem. Indeed, Christ was rejected by His own people, a fact which made the Apostle Paul declare: "There is no eternal city for us in this life" (Heb 13:11–14), and how true it is that the disciple is not above his Master!

55. *Crucifixion of Christ.* Master Dionysius, late 15th-early 16th c.
Cathedral of the Trinity of Obnorski Monastery. Tretiakov Gallery, Moscow.

The white linen draped gracefully over His loins reinforces the beauty of the ensemble, which is so full of harmony and rhythm. The Cross stands out against the light of the golden background.

Permeated with the leaven of Paschal joy, sadness fails to dominate the scene; for here the Glory of God truly reigns.

4. *The icon of the Resurrection or the Descent into Hell*

Orthodoxy witnesses strongly to the Resurrection, which constitutes the principal theme of the liturgy of Vespers each Saturday, and of Orthros (Matins) each Sunday morning. The faithful who come to church on Sundays almost always participate at the Office of the Resurrection. "The Feast of Feasts," its icon quite naturally assumes a very special meaning.

Contrary to the precise and numerous details we have at our disposal about the Crucifixion, the evangelists say nothing about the exact moment of the Resurrection of Jesus. It would hardly have been possible to capture the moment, as for instance at the resurrection of Lazarus, who came forth from his tomb right in front of his family and friends. The Resurrection is an event impossible for us to gauge, and consequently it is beyond any kind of scientific analysis; yet in spite of this, it nevertheless remains an authentic historical fact, an essential landmark in our history. Let us qualify this by saying that it is not an historical fact in the strict sense of secular history, but rather a theological fact and reality that transcends our human, historical possibilities.

Even if eyewitnesses of the exact moment of the Resurrection are lacking, there are still certain bystanders who attest to the fact, beginning with the guards at His tomb. Orthodoxy does not try to represent the actual moment of the Resurrection when Christ rose from His tomb, because to do this deforms truth and destroys the mystery.

Tradition admits two icons of the Resurrection in conformity with the Sacred Scriptures: the icon of the Holy Myrrhbearing Women (cf. p. 120) at the tomb (Mt 28:1–8), and that of the Descent of Christ into Hades, which we have chosen here as an illustration.

The iconographic theme of this very beautiful icon was established already in the eighth century; the inscription *"Anastasis,"* i.e., "the rising"—from the "Fall"—is often written on it. Without any doubt, its content owes much to the apocryphal Gospel of Nicodemus mentioned earlier.

56. *Harrowing of Hell.* Fresco of the monastery of Moldovita, 1537.
Moldovita, Romania (Photo: Michel and Lieselotte Quenot).

Flashing like a burst of lightning, Christ appears in Hades as the Master of life and of the cosmos. Victorious over death's abyss, His glorious body is vivified by His divinity. His body now radiates Divine Energies, symbolized in the golden rays; the expression of this Divine dynamism is repeated by His fluttering robes. "Indescribable Light," His entire Being announces the bright dawn of a new day. Having broken the gates of Hell, spread in the form of a cross over the abyss, Christ tramples them underfoot and grasps the hand of Adam, whom He vigorously delivers from the darkness of death.

This face-to-face meeting of the first and Second Adam assumes a special meaning. The icon unites with the Byzantine liturgy in strongly stressing that the rising of Christ announces the good news of the Resurrection to all humanity. Hence, there is a close relation between the silhouette of the Risen Christ and that of Adam, whom He carries off into the glory of His Resurrection. With Adam, it is all humanity—his posterity—which is included. Exhausted after having been wakened from the sleep of spiritual death, Adam stares at His liberator with a look of joy still marked by fatigue. He holds up his free hand in a gesture of welcome and of prayer, drawn toward His Creator just as a flower is drawn toward the sun. In the foreground we also see the kneeling Eve timidly raise her hands covered with an edge of her cloak. Behind her are often seen Moses carrying the Tablets of the Law, the righteous, and those prophets who have announced the arrival of the Savior.

On the left, clothed in robes of royalty, stand David and Solomon, prayerful and welcoming; behind them are a prophet and John the Forerunner, sent to Hades to announce the arrival of the Master of Life. With a movement of his hand John points out Christ, who often holds a Cross, the instrument of His victory. Nails, bolts and locks litter the black hole of hell, whose entrance is surrounded by confining mountains. Christ glorified, transfigured in a spiritual body, escapes the laws of this world whose gravity engenders death and corruptibility. As leader of the human race, He has become forever absolute transparency, openness and communion.

A quick glance back at the icon of Christ's Nativity now gives us a better idea of the significant parallels existing between the two feasts: both of them can be called "Pascha." The Child-God is born mystically in the heart of Hades. "Torch-bearer of Light, the flesh of God beneath the earth

57. *Descent into Hell.* Russian, 15th c.
Compliments, Temple Gallery London.
(Photo: St. Vladimir's Seminary Press S–328)

58. *Christ Pantocrator.* 20th c. by Monk Gregory Kroug.
Montgeron, Paris.
(Photo: Andrew Tregubov)

59a, b, c, d. A montage showing the grotto and its symbolism.
Details from the icon of the Deisis and the Great Feasts.
(Photo: Michel and Lieselotte Quenot)

dissipates the darkness of Hades," proclaims the liturgy of the Nativity, which is echoed again at Matins of Holy Saturday: "You descended to earth to save Adam and not finding him, O Master, you went down into Hades to look for him." The Nativity thus heralds the Resurrection; in a way, it even includes it. Does not the Divine Child lie in the cavern wrapped in swaddling bands which are similar to the bands of Lazarus who was raised from the dead? The dark cavern is an image of hell, which we find again in the icon of the Baptism of Jesus, where the Jordan River is transformed into a watery tomb, an element of the cosmos which is purified by His body. Nor should we forget the black grotto we see beneath the Cross in the icon of the Crucifixion.

The entire Old Testament anticipates the arrival of Christ. His Incarnation and Resurrection are its final accomplishment and fulfillment. Both of these mysteries reveal God to us in the very heart of our history, and they illuminate everything:

> Be not afraid, it is I, the First and the Last. I am the Living One, I was dead and now I am to live for ever and ever, and I hold the keys of death and of the underworld. (Rev 1:17–18)

As seen in this icon, Christ also descends into the depths of our being to free us from the darkness of evil. Our union with the Crucified-Resurrected requires that we be "buried with him by baptism into His death" (Col 2:12)—from whence comes the ancient, meaningful rite of immersion—so that we may rise with Him from the dead.

"Give your blood and receive the Spirit": words from Tradition which sweep aside any ambiguity. Eternal life postulates the death of the "old man" by an abandoning and a transcending of that original evil which threatens us daily. Tangible consequences of that dark stain are evident in our worries, limitations, failures, blindness to others through our egotism, and shortsightedness before the beauty of creation. Yet everything is caught up in a liberating ascent, to the extent that we accept Christ crucified and risen, who alone helps us "pass over" (Pascha = Passover) from the dark empire of death, to Light, the source of all Life!

4

Theological Elements of the Icon

1. The icon: an image which purifies

Images flood our lives. They triumph today in every social milieu: in our streets, at work, even in the heart of our homes through newspapers, magazines, and the TV screen. Media technicians are quite familiar with the habits these engender; they respond by using presentations and colors ever more subtle and insistent, with little consideration at all for the sensitivity of the audience they try to cajole.

Because of their suggestiveness, images can be used against us without our even realizing it. They can prejudice our thoughts, enflame our passions, influence our behavior: in a word, they are capable of depriving us of our personal freedom. In today's society, pictures tend more and more to replace written text. The result is that our thinking process easily surrenders to "feelings" and above all to whatever we look at. Take for example the influence of enticing visual attractions offered daily in our streets from store windows, displays, and their bright, flashing neon lights! And what should we say about the invasion from every direction of visual publicity geared to profit? We must honestly admit that when the profit motive takes over, human values are discarded, because we listen to the greedy call of our senses far more readily. Images and pictures manage to worm their way into the very depths of our souls by their highly suggestive, symbolic force; their impact on our sensibilities at the same threatens time our interior life.

In a civilization influenced by pictures and an omnipresent material-ism, our post-industrial society is undergoing a profound crisis. Personal freedom, just as that of an artist, authorizes us to transform the world according to our image and conception of things. If our vision and perspective are untarnished, we can spiritualize everything. But if the contrary is true, then we remain prisoners confined to the influences of matter, space and time.

60. *The Prophet Elijah in the Desert.* Russian (Novgorod), late 15th c.
Icon Museum, Recklinghausen, Germany.
(Photo: Recklinghausen Museum)

The entire spiritual life postulates a choice between these two centers: either the "corporealization of the soul," or the "spiritualization of the body" in the way shown to us by the icon.

Should we not admit that our present rationalistic, scientific and technical exclusiveness is being paid for with a perilous atrophy of our general faculties? Does not the irrelevancy of modern paintings offer us numerous examples and clear proof of this fact? The sight of our world transformed into a gigantic garbage can—offered by certain contemporary artists as "art"—only serves to demonstrate the miasmas of their subconscious.

"When souls start to break down, then faces also degenerate," wrote the great Russian author Nicholas Gogol, who emphasized how every artist is invested with a mission he should not ignore:

Art reconciles us with life. Art is the introduction of order and harmony into the soul, not of trouble and disorder… If an artist does not accomplish the miracle of transforming the soul of the spectator into an attitude of love and forgiveness, then his art is only an ephemeral passion. (Extract from a letter to the poet Zhukovskii; January 1, 1848)

Humanity is influenced progressively by what it contemplates. We discover among Tibetans and Cambodians the characteristic calmness and serenity of Buddha, whose image has profoundly influenced them.

The lamp of your body is your eye. When your eye is sound, your whole body too is filled with light; but when it is diseased, your body too will be darkness. (Lk 11:34)

This verse of St Luke's Gospel brings us back to the icon. It is a source of purification and an apprenticeship which helps us develop our interior vision. As we have already pointed out, the ancient Fathers of the Church considered our sight as the most important of our senses, and images as a means of sanctification for the soul.

An icon is certainly not the image of a disincarnate world—in the sense that it would refuse creation. Rather, it is the image of a world transformed, transfigured, rendered transparent by a spiritualization which embraces the entire cosmos.

The icon of Christ, "The Image not made by hands," is the basic model for every other representation of the human face. This face of God-become-man sanctifies the faces of all humanity: black, white, red, yellow, and mixed races of every color. Consequently, whoever refuses to recognize a reflection of the Divine Face in the face of another human being becomes an iconoclast. He or she is Cain living and acting all over again!

It seems appropriate for us to add here that the essential outlook of a Christian artist and painter does not reside in painting abstract forms, but rather in a rediscovery of the human face, since the Incarnation of Christ—true God and true man—postulates this very fact.

The icon fulfills our vision of a universe of beauty by being a representation of transcendent reality. Meditation finds an excellent aid in the icon, which keeps our mind on the image and helps us concentrate on the symbolized reality.

It is something similar to the meeting of the Prophet Elijah with God that we read about in the First Book of Kings: "...There came a mighty wind... but the Eternal One was not in the wind. After the wind came an earthquake. But the Eternal One was not in the earthquake. After the earthquake came a fire. But the Eternal One was not in the fire. After the fire there came the sound of a gentle breeze..." (1 Kings 19:12–13), announcing the presence of the Eternal One.

2. The Incarnation

The essential element involved in the veneration of icons is our witnessing to the Incarnation. We must go even further by saying that the icon of Christ participates in the person of the Model, thus prolonging His Incarnation. According to Leonid Ouspensky, the icon is "a visible proof of both the abasement of God towards humanity as well as of the élan or impetus of humanity towards God"; and for Monk Gregory it is "visible and tangible evidence of the grafting of created humanity onto the Divine Uncreated Being."

In his treatise *On the defense of icons*, written in the eighth century, St John of Damascus used strong words:

I do not adore matter, but I adore the Creator of matter, who became matter for my sake, who willed to take His abode in matter; who worked out my salvation through matter which saved me, (because God) saved humanity by one of our own. He assumed a totally human nature and is thus united fully to humanity, so that He who is both true God and true man might bring us His salvation.

61. *The Transfiguration of Christ.* Painted in the 1970's in Russia.
French crypt of the Patriarchal Orthodox Centre, Geneva-Chambésy, Switzerland.
(Photo: Michel and Lieselotte Quenot)

His stressing the Incarnation of God should not surprise us. The entire economy of our salvation is based on this mystery. To forget it or to deny it would provoke a rapid collapse of the Church and its Faith.

In the second century, St Irenaeus made the following statement, which has since become a sort of theological slogan for us: "If the Word of God became incarnate, it was so that mankind might also be deified" (*Against Heresies,* V, pref., PG, col 1035).

Christ does not destroy time, He fulfills it and redeems it. Does not St Paul write to the Romans that "all creation is eagerly waiting for the revelation of the sons of God" (Rom 8:15)? In plain language, this means that if the entire material world, the cosmos, inherits our human destiny tainted by sin, it is the sincere Christian's obligation to help liberate it from sin and evil. So it becomes our task to spiritualize the matter we use every day to help further restore all creation to God (cf. Eph 1:9–10).

Biblical and Christian Tradition define idolatry as a transference of our contemplation, love and worship of God to things which are material and worldly. Beauty, originally destined to encourage our approach to Supreme Beauty, which is God Himself, has presently become an end in itself—need we mention our continual "Miss" pageants and "Mr." competitions, or the movie star, music hall and sports "idols" with whom youth and too many adults become so beguiled? Today more than ever, the icon permits us to resume once again that original contemplation of beauty and to accomplish a veritable reverse transference, since the goal of the Incarnation is to re-orient humanity and our outlook towards God.

The Incarnation of Christ becomes a beacon illuminating every aspect and instant of Christian life. In light of the Incarnation, even the most simple actions in life, whether eating or drinking, rising or sleeping—just the very fact of living—are capable of transfiguration and discover their profound meaning in the liturgy (cf. St Paul: 1 Cor 10:31). And when liturgy is mentioned in this context, it must always be because of the integration of the icon into the liturgical mystery itself, for Paul Evdokimov calls the liturgy "the icon of the entire economy of our salvation."

3. The Transfiguration

The Transfiguration is at the heart of the icon because it is the keystone of Byzantine doctrines concerning the vision of God. The icon is indeed a vision of God made man and of His deifying grace manifested in men. It is the prototype and not just the portrait of our future *transfigured* humanity; it expresses the new order of the cosmos, where beasts and mankind live together in harmony. We have already mentioned examples of saints who lived near wild animals, which would come to lick their hands in a friendly manner as if tamed by the saint.

But the transfiguration that awaits all humanity, including necessarily our bodies, according to the Fathers of the Church, is announced in the Transfiguration of Christ on Mount Tabor proclaimed in the Gospels: "There He was transfigured before them: His face shone like the sun and His clothes became as white as light" (Mt 17:2; Mk 9:1–8; Lk 9:27–36). We shall better understand that this God-like form is *the* state to which every human being is called if we read the following passage of the Evangelist Matthew more carefully: "Then the righteous will shine like the sun in the Kingdom of their Father" (13:43).

At our creation, the image of God was deeply engraved in us, but it was defaced by the Fall of our first parents. It is restored to us again by our participation in the Incarnation of Christ, and above all by our Baptism. Yet our resemblance to God results from our acquiring the Holy Spirit, which is realized according to each person's capacity (1 Cor 15:41–43).

People represented in an icon are filled with divine grace. By their participation in the divine life, they sanctify space, time and everything that surrounds them. Freed from human passions, they represent that complete fullness of their deified, transfigured human nature. The deification of a saint diffuses itself, permitting us to speak of a transfiguration of the cosmos. The icon, being a "vision of God," should inspire prayer in whoever contemplates it. We must note that, in Orthodoxy, the true theologian is above all the one who has a personal experience of God. Since it rejects any realism whatsoever, the icon requires its spectator to approach a different sort of vision; we are personally invited to participate in this transfiguration. Let us come back to the account by Motovilov about the transfiguration of Seraphim of Sarov (†1833):

"Your face has become brighter than the sun. It hurts my eyes…"

Father Seraphim said:

"Do not be afraid, lover of God, because you are now as radiant as myself. You

62. *St. Seraphim of Sarov.* 20th c. by Monk Gregory Kroug.
Montgeron, Paris.
(Photo: Andrew Tregubov)

too are in the fullness of the Spirit of God, because otherwise you could not see me in this state!"

This testimony underlines two realities: the action of the Holy Spirit and the light resulting from His presence. But every icon speaks about Divine Energy and about light; it thus repeats the liturgy of the Church which sings: "Thy light shines on the faces of Thy saints."

4. Light: "brilliantly shining darkness"

Since light is the very first attribute of God (Ps 27:1; Is 60:19–20; 42:6) should we be surprised at this section's heading? The icon of the Nativity shows us Christ as a spot of light piercing the darkness of the grotto. The same is true of the Resurrection icon, where His dazzling silhouette radiates like lightning in the dark of the night. He is the "Light of the world" about whom the prologue of the Johannine Gospel speaks, and whom the Evangelist Luke calls the "Light to enlighten the nations" (Lk 2:32).

But the four symbols of light, seen in the rays, in the gold hatching lines (assist), the nimbus, and the white garments, capture our attention particularly in the icon of the Transfiguration. The rays recall the brilliance of the sun, the gold hatching lines symbolize the resplendency of the Divine Life; the nimbus, used in other traditions to enhance the head, in turn evokes the solar sphere as a symbolic image of the sacred and of that spiritual energy which it radiates. As for the white garments, they represent purity, incorruptibility—in a word, absolute perfection.

The illumination of humanity is nothing more than the "divinization" (*theosis*) about which the Fathers of the Church frequently speak. Hence, the affirmation of that great Father of the Church, Gregory Palamas (†1359), for whom participation in the Divine Energy leads a person to become, in a certain way, himself *light*.

The people seen in icons are penetrated with Uncreated Light and participate intimately in the life of God, because, "having approached Light itself, the soul is transfigured into light" (St Gregory of Nyssa).

Light plays a primary role in nature and likewise in every civilization; life depends upon it, as well as happiness. Our entire existence hinges on the polarity of day and night, which is also expressed quite well by the dualism of ancient China called "Yin-Yang." The Greek Hades or Hell, "Sheol" in Hebrew, is nothing else than a dark place where solitude reigns. Light permits us to see the other person, to establish that mutual recognition necessary for every personal relationship.

Night, on the contrary, symbolizes evil, death, darkness. Do we not sometimes say of night: "it's pitch-dark out tonight"? Darkness implies the absence of light, while an intense luminosity makes light and translucence.

Light can be called the "mother" of colors; it plays an extremely important role in art. How could we fail to mention those great pensive artists like Rembrandt, La Tour, or Corot, whose luminous canvases seem to shine from the depths? Such self-illumination implies the use of an illusory light that contrasts with the art of the icon, where light is neither artificially created nor projected from the exterior. Light in the icon sparkles through purified beings, as we are reminded by the golden background, symbol of Divine Light itself, Creator of everything.

In antiquity there was already a developed system of physics about sight. The theory is simple: both the eye and the object emit their own light. There is, in a sense, sight or vision whenever the eye and the object attain the same frequency, or better yet, meet at the same point. The result is a communication between the one who sees and that which is seen. What is interesting in this conception—even if it is questionable—is the fact that it agrees with other later theories confirming the idea that vision or sight transforms. In the third century, the philosopher Plotinus describes how man escapes from the world of matter by light. He refers to an interior light, invisible to our human eyes, which requires vision from the Spirit. Natural light, seen with our human eyes, becomes darkness through its submission to matter. Hence the disconcerting expression of Dionysius the Areopagite (sixth century), who speaks of God as being "brilliantly shining darkness." The icons of the Transfiguration and of the Harrowing of Hell represent Christ in white garments or clothed in gold, shining with light. His glorified body is often drawn in three or four concentric circles symbolizing Divine Light. Furthermore, each circle is painted in a darker tone as it approaches the blue center, which is often midnight blue. By losing its luminosity, natural light spiritualizes, and darkness becomes light.

If man is "transformed" by what he contemplates, then the light from beyond, which emanates from the icon, penetrates to the very depths of his being.

> The soul which has been perfectly illuminated by that indescribable beauty of the luminous glory of the face of Christ and filled with the Holy Spirit... is all eye, all light, all face. (Macarius the Great, *Homily* 1, 2, PG 34, 451 AB)

Holos Ophtalmos... All eye! This is the invitation of an old desert Father, Abba Bessarion, who lived at the beginning of the fifth century. Although blind toward the end of his life, his eyes seemed to be extremely large and transparent. Shortly before dying, he told a young novice who had come for spiritual direction that a monk ought to be like the cherubim and seraphim: *Holos Ophtalmos.*

The considerable use of gold as the background for icons can now be better appreciated, because contrary to colors, gold does not come from light, it is light.

5. Presence and Encounter

According to St Gregory the Great, "icons are for the unlettered what the Sacred Scriptures are for the instructed" (*Letter to Serenus*, Bishop of Marseille, PL 77, 1027). However well-known, this statement, taken out of context, is incomplete, because even if the icon has a pastoral and an undeniably pedagogical value, it is above all a *personal encounter* with the Holy Spirit in the person represented (Nicaea II), which Leonid Ouspensky expresses thus:

> It is the grace of the Holy Spirit which sanctifies the person represented as well as the icon itself, and it is there that the relation between the faithful and the saint occurs through the intermediary of the icon.

In his book from which we have already quoted, Sergius Bulgakov writes:

> Orthodoxy believes the icon is a dwelling place of God's grace, like an epiphany or manifestation of Christ (of the Theotokos, or of the Saints) in general, of the person it portrays; and thus we may pray before it... a blessing may be communicated by the icon, as if coming from those represented on it.

The icon sanctifies the place where it is located and creates for the faithful a tangible sense of the Divine Presence. It is most certainly an "encounter," because to pray before an icon of Christ is to pray in His

63. *Archangel Michael.* From Deisis, Rublev influence, 16th c.
Castle de Wijenburgh, Echteld, Netherlands.
(Photo: St Vladimir's Seminary Press S–151)

64. *St. John the Baptist.* Byzantine, school of Constantinople, late 14th c.
Compliments, Temple Gallery, London.
(Photo: St Vladimir's Seminary Press S–160)

presence. While the Eucharist—being Christ Himself—does not convey His personal likeness based upon the external appearance of the bread and wine, the icon does convey His likeness based on the personal identity with the prototype, yet remains clearly distinct from Him according to nature.

6. The Christian: a living icon

"The glory of God is mankind," says the Talmud, and St Irenaeus also repeated these same words in the second century. "Created in the image and likeness of God" (Gen 2:27), mankind, beginning with Adam, by the Fall defaced the divine reflection that God had bestowed upon him.

We become sons of God with Christ through His incarnation, and both His death and resurrection strengthen our filiation by grace. The veil of the Temple torn through the middle (Lk 23:5) stresses the fact that humanity is no longer separated from God. Since the Risen Christ is the image of the Father, a Christian who contemplates the Savior and purifies himself progressively becomes an icon of God.

The Greek Fathers of the Church often make the distinction between the *image* of God and *resemblance* to God. Origen wrote the following words:

> Man received the privilege of the image of God at his creation, but the total perfection of a resemblance to God will be conferred on him only when all things are fulfilled.

The image of God was given along with the breath of life, while the resemblance to God marks the goal of our earthly pilgrimage. It is the crown of life offered to the blessed in the heavenly Kingdom.

Earlier in this book, we stated that man thirsts for beauty. The beauty of which mankind is intrinsically the image is none other than God Himself; our entire being yearns for Him. If God is the intimate center of our being, both our humanity and our sense of the human are nonetheless "conditioned" and limited by our sense of the Divine. To state that the death of Christ entails our death too means precisely that, and nothing more. Man is an icon of God, but only insofar as he is fully human, radiating the presence of Christ.

Holos Ophtalmos! Does that not imply a complete openness to every

person, to the cosmos, and to God? Olivier Clément puts it quite well
when he writes:

> Christianity is the religion of faces... To be a Christian is to discover, even at
> the very heart of nothingness and of death, a face which is forever open like a
> door of light—the Face of Christ—and surrounding Him, penetrated with His
> light, His tenderness, the faces of sinners who have been forgiven and who no
> longer judge others, but simply welcome them into their hearts. The word
> "Gospel," (Godspel) means the proclamation of the joy of the "Good News"!

The icon is a model of holiness, of presence, and a revelation of the
cosmic transfiguration to come; it offers itself to all of us like a beautiful
open book. But we must know how to read the icon to be able really to
see those faces we pass every day in our streets and discover in them that
"unique plant" grafted onto Christ, the Tree of Life.

To restore a face to those "without a face" (*aprosopos*) is the icon's
invitation to all of us, repeated by Didymus of Alexandria: "After God, see
God in every man and woman..."

Let us conclude this final chapter with the following remark: during
our long pilgrimage across the Holy Mountain Athos, we were struck by
the profound similarity between the faces painted in the marvelous Byzantine frescoes of the churches and refectories, and the faces of several
monks we met there. Nourished with the same Living Water, their eye
oriented toward the same light, they radiate the light of the Sun.

Conclusion

I conography is a theological art consisting of both the vision and knowledge of God. Neither art nor theology taken separately could create an icon; the union of both is necessary. Based on the Incarnation, of which it is a constant reminder, its rich theology of forms and colors is closely related to the other forms of theology. Living from Tradition as it does, the icon permits us to return to our origins and roots. And while spiritual decadence was bound up with its rapid decline, the present spiritual renewal apparent here and there quite often owes much to the icon.

Today, humanity finds itself at a crossroad in history, where a new culture in gestation is undergoing the problems and pains of birth. Our present era is totally anthropocentric. It is breaking all records for the number of organizations geared to the promotion—the safeguard—of human rights, and especially for people's "well-being." And yet, these very same rights are flouted daily in the majority of countries around the world, while vital problems for the future survival of humanity, as well as of our natural environment, daily come into focus with an increasing precision and urgency as never before in the past. The icon, however, reveals to us a world of beauty, harmony and peace, where humanity and the cosmos together can rediscover something of their Edenic state of living. For an art and a world so often wrapped-up in themselves, to the point of forming a prison of immanence, as it were, the icon substitutes transcendence, with an openness toward the beyond as the only possible solution for the happiness of all. In fact, icons constantly remind us about the finality of our human existence, that we must become *ophthalmos*, eye, to develop an interior vision nourished by the Holy Spirit who transfigures everything. Since the icon finds its creative principle in the light of Christ's Transfiguration, it invites all of us to reflect this transfiguration in the world by welcoming the Holy Spirit within us, which is the very goal of Christian life, according to St Seraphim of Sarov.

The Acts of the Apostles relate how St Paul was shocked at the sight of so many idols in the city of Athens. However, he was surprised and happy to discover an altar bearing the inscription: "To an Unknown God" (Acts 17:23). Is it not this "Unknown God" which art seeks in its repetitions of shadows and lights? Indeed, we must recover a purified vision, and free ourselves of our "cataract"—an excessive materialism creating "idols" which make us prisoners of our own little world. There is no doubt, art truly reflects life! To reconcile ourselves with God, to rediscover and then to develop our spiritual vision and outlook, this is what the icon humbly invites us to do.

Over the centuries, historical developments with far-reaching conse-quences have taken place in the two original cradles of the icon, Byzan-tium and Russia. Both countries have lost either totally or partially the Christianity which owes so much to them. Even though steeped in transcendence, Islam, which now occupies Constantinople, bases its icon-oclasm on an ignorance of the Divine Incarnation. As for Russia—revived by the prayers and the blood of so many, many martyrs—may it redis-cover its stability through a unity of all which respects every "person," as is so beautifully suggested in Rublev's icon of the Trinity.

Because it is so profoundly engraved in the hearts of the Russian people, the icon will inevitably reappear one of these days with renewed force, as numerous signs of the times have manifested these past few years.

The icon accompanies Orthodox faithful from their cradle to their grave. When confined to a museum, it no longer fulfills its primary function. Uprooted and reduced to being an object of art, it still preserves, at least we think so, its spiritual energies accumulated down the centuries by generations of the faithful who have prayed before it. Cherished for its antiquity and for its beauty, the icon continues to be a silent witness to a transfigured world.

Prudence is needed today in face of a proliferation of icon reproduc-tions on paper or made by other commercial procedures. Surely, if there exist fine copies glued on a board of solid wood ordinarily made in monastic workshops, too many of these cheap copies often empty the icon of its heart and soul. We have already pointed out the importance of both the wooden board and the materials used for its support, as well as the colors and the backgrounds. All of these elements are things that cheap paper reproductions cannot match.

How can we not be disturbed when we learn about icon courses organized in various places offering neophytes the possibility of painting an icon within a very short time? And how many people today, interested in iconography, are satisfied with only a rudimentary introduction before they begin on their own as "iconographers." In truth, an authentic apprenticeship requires a prolonged, arduous commitment over several years and tutoring by a master iconographer before the title "iconographer" can be claimed. Icons are a patrimony of the undivided Church; but following the schism they have been transmitted to us only by the Orthodox Church, whose sacred, liturgical images they have remained to the present. Non-Orthodox Christians eager to resume this art must first assimilate the liturgical life maintained by Orthodox Tradition, share its prayer and belief. If they do not approach the icon in this manner, then invariably they will distort its nature, and torn from its roots it will end up becoming just another "holy picture"(in the Roman Catholic sense of the term), which it precisely *is not*! Should we not also regret a growing tendency among certain people to invite children to paint "their" icon? Almost as soon as it is discovered, the icon is misunderstood and reduced to being another "holy picture" because it has been separated from its sacred aspect.

We must once again insist on the fact that icon painting demands an artistic talent plus the daily living of an intense spiritual life in the Church, itself nutured by Tradition. An authentic iconographer is—must be—a theologian of the image, because iconography is a language which, to speak it well, implies a living Faith.

In the aftermath of its loss of unity which began in the seventeenth century, the nineteenth-century icon often abandoned its canonical character and ceased to be part of the great iconographic Tradition. This explains the presence of non-iconic images in many Orthodox churches even though a faithful allegiance to the icon is recognized as being essential. Forcing the facts somewhat, we can say that a disoriented Western Christianity in search of norms and forms for its sacred imagery, is rediscovering the icon with a certain fervor, even if at times rather tactlessly as a result of a multi-secular separation. It faces an Orthodox East whose iconography has been altered for the worse by Renaissance art, although happily still preserved in the perennial context of its liturgical life. Such art in Orthodoxy needs to re-orient itself with an iconography revived according to the great Tradition and inspired by the breath of the Holy Spirit.

However, we rejoice at the present day iconographic renewal; above all we are comforted by the fact that Russian immigrants in France, such as Gregory Kroug (†1969) and Leonid Ouspensky (†1987), have so remarkably contributed to our generation. Greece is following in the footsteps of Photius Kontoglou (†1965), to whom goes the credit for having initiated a revival of the Byzantine tradition in his country, entrusting to his successors an extremely detailed manual for the use of iconographers. As creators of this art, and consequently heirs to the charism of all originators, the Greeks seem to be demonstrating a greater dynamism in iconographic renewal (disregarding the kitsch all too often provided for tourists) than the Russians, who are nevertheless full of potential. Yet it is quite true that in large part, although not exclusively, the most beautiful icons found in the West originate from Russia—a Russia, ironic as it may seem given its recent past, that continues to evangelize a spiritually undernourished West in its own special way.

Within the fraternal dialogue inaugurated between Christians, the icon is a privileged meeting place, a genuine leaven of unity. But it must be discovered or re-discovered according to the criteria we have presented here, i.e., in a traditional iconographic purity which expresses the profound truths of faith.

There are a certain number of things in theology which the language of words simply cannot express, but iconography in its purest tradition permits this maximal approach to those mysteries. Oriented toward the same goal, sacred Byzantine or Slavonic music is closely linked to icons. It gives meaning to the words set to it, endowing them with a dynamism that would otherwise be unattainable.

Finally, we must remember that the icon is much more than a form of teaching or an aid for prayer: it is an object for our veneration. An icon which is no longer venerated is like a diamond deprived of light; it no longer seems to radiate, yet it is always ready to sparkle with fire at the slightest ray of sunlight!

Amid the surfeit of images swamping our world today, the icon testifies to the spiritual outlook and vision of an authentic Christianity, that of the Divine Humanity of Christ. Its language of love is revealed when eyes meet. It not only imperceptibly enriches and fructifies every face that gazes at it, but contains the vivifying impulse that leads to the joyful rediscovery of a Christian, theological art.

A window on the Kingdom, the icon allows us to see both light and beauty from the invisible world that would otherwise blind our eyes. It does not just open onto the world beyond, but lets in that vital air which refreshes our hearts.

Steeped in a faith that seeks theophany, the icon challenges all of us, revealing itself in the silence of a face-to-face. We must "listen" to it, so that it may manifest the Word (Jn 1:14).

Selection of Museums and Collections of Icons

Bulgaria: Sofia, National Gallery and Crypt of the Alexander Nevsky Cathedral.

Canada: Ottawa, The National Gallery; Toronto, Royal Ontario Museum.

Crete: Heraklion, Agia Aikaterini.

Cyprus: Kyrenia, Metropolitan Palace; Nicosia, Phaneromini collection; Paphos, Byzantine Museum.

Czechoslovakia: Bardejov, Slovakia, Sarisske Muzeum.

Egypt: Cairo, The Coptic Museum; Mount Sinai, St Catherine's Monastery.

England: London, Victoria and Albert Museum.

Finland: Helsinki, The National Museum.

France: Paris, The Louvre.

Germany: Recklinghausen, Icon Museum.

Greece: Athens, The Benaki and The Byzantine Museums; Meteora, the five monasteries open to the public, above all the Transfiguration monastery; Mount Athos, especially the following monasteries: Chilandari, Dionysiou, Docheiariou, Great Lavra, Iviron, Stavronikita and Vatopedi.

Holland: Echtel, Wijenburgh Castle icon collection.

Ireland: Dublin, The National Gallery.

Italy: Ravenna, Byzantine Museum; Rome, Vatican, The Pinacotheca (Byzantine section); Venice, Hellenic Institute and Church of San Giorgio dei Greci.

Jerusalem: Greek Orthodox Patriarchate.

Norway: Oslo, National Gallery.

Patmos: St John's Monastery.

Poland: Krakow, National Museum.

Rhodes: Metropolitan Palace.

Rumania: Bucharest, Art Museum.

Russia: Moscow, Tretiakov Gallery, Andrei Rublev Museum, Kremlin Museum, National Museum of History, Pushkin Museum of art, Cathedrals of the Annunciation, the Dormition and St Michael. Kiev, Museum of Russian Art, Cathedral of St Sophia. Leningrad, The Hermitage (Byzantine section), Russian National Museum. Novgorod, Museum of Art and History, Church of the Transfiguration. Vologda, Russian Museum. Iaroslav, Art Museum. Zagorsk, Cathedral and Museum of Art.

Sweden: Stockholm, National Museum.

Switzerland: Kölliken, private collection of Dr. Siegfried Amberg-Herzog.

Turkey: Constantinople (Istanbul), Ecumenical Patriarchate.

U.S.A.: Baltimore, MD., Walters Art Gallery; Ligonier, PA., Antiochian Village Collection; New York City, Metropolitan Museum of Art; Princeton, NJ., The Art Museum; Santa Barbara, CA., Santa Barbara Museum of Art; Passaic, NJ., The Heritage Center, Diocese of Passaic; Washington D.C., Dumbarton Oaks Collection.

Yugoslavia: Belgrade, National Museum, Museum of the Orthodox Serbian Church. Ochrid, Churches of St Sophia and St Clement with Museum. Skoplje, Gallery of Fine Arts.

Select Bibliography

Baggley, John, *Doors of Perception: Icons and Their Spiritual Significance* (Crestwood: St Vladimir's Seminary Press, 1988).

Basil, St, *On the Holy Spirit*, D. Anderson, trans. (Crestwood: St Vladimir's Seminary Press, 1980).

Bulgakov Sergius, *The Orthodox Church.* L. Kesich, trans (Crestwood: St Vladimir's Seminary Press, 1988).

Clément, Olivier, *Le Visage Intérieur* (Stock, 1978).

Dionysius of Fourna, *The Painter's Manual,* P. Hetherington, trans. (Oakwood Publications, 1989).

Evdokimov, Paul, *The Art of the Icon: A Theology of Beauty* (Oakwood Publications, 1990).

Grabar, André, *La Peinture Byzantine* (Genève: Skira, 1979).

Itten J., *L'art de la Couleur* (Paris: Dessain et Tolra, 1975).

John of Damascus, St, *On the Divine Images*, D. Anderson, trans. (Crestwood: St Vladimir's Seminary Press, 1980).

Kalokyris, Constantine D., *The Essence of Orthodox Iconography* (Brookline: Holy Cross Orthodox Press, 1971).

Kroug, Grégoire, *Carnets d'un peintre d'icônes* (Lausanne: L'âge d'homme, 1983).

Ouspensky, Leonid, *Theology of the Icon* (Crestwood: St Vladimir's Seminary Press, 1978).

_____, *The Theology of the Icon,* vol. I and II (Crestwood: St Vladimir's Seminary Press, 1991).

Ouspensky L. and Lossky V., *The Meaning of Icons* (Crestwood: St Vladimir's Seminary Press, 1982).

Philokalia, Palmer, Sherrard, Ware, trans. (London: Faber and Faber, 1979; vol. 2, 1981; vol. 3, 1984).

Sendler, Egon, *The Icon: Image of the Invisible*, S. Bigham, trans. (Oakwood Publications, 1988).

Theodore the Studite, St, *On the Holy Icons*, Catharine P. Roth, trans. (Crestwood: St Vladimir's Seminary Press, 1981).

Tregubov, Andrew, *The Light of Christ: Iconography of Gregory Kroug* (Crestwood: St Vladimir's Seminary Press, 1990).

Trubetskoy, Eugene N., *Icons: Theology in Color* (Crestwood: St Vladimir's Seminary Press, 1973).

Zander, Valentine, *St Seraphim of Sarov* (Crestwood: St Vladimir's Seminary Press, 1975).

Index

List of Plates*

*Asterisk indicates color plates.